30 Real Christ...

True life experiences wi.   **ime**

By MJ ⌐ land

"There coils a fear beneath the loveliest dream."
T.Watts

Paperback published November 2021
ISBN: 9798495516946

Copyright © 2021 MJ Wayland
All Artwork Copyright © 2021 L.Jeffrey

Published by Sarkless Kitty

Author website
www.mjwayland.com

Artist website
https://ghestwyck.com

Contents

Foreword

Christmas is such a paradoxical season; on one hand, it's a time of family gatherings and giving presents. Yet, it is a time of increased curiosity into the strange and weird stories that haunt us.

In writing this book, I decided to explore and evaluate some of the incredible ghost stories that litter the archives of libraries of Britain and the United States. Out of the hundreds of anecdotes and references I uncovered, I have brought a collection of Christmas ghost stories, keeping as close to the original sources as possible.

Many of the stories have never seen print since the original experiences. As well as stories that have not seen print in over a hundred years, I have been able to bring new light to two classic cases, Calverley Old Hall and the East Barnet Hauntings. The former is an incredibly haunting tale of a small village in Yorkshire said to be haunted by a child murderer, and the latter is a tale from more recent times in which a knight in armour terrorises a London Park at Christmas.

But why is Christmas, well, so haunted? Many researchers link Christmas with the pagan festival of Yule on December 20th, but two other pagan festivals have links to Christian festivals as well. Halloween, or Samhain for pagans and Wiccans, is the day before All Saint's Day on November the first and Beltane before the 1st May Christian feast day. Manvers Moore wrote in 1849,

> The Eve of Christmas indeed seems to be a
> favourite time for evil spirits of every unpleasant
> type, eager to do as much as they can before the
> Holy Day dawn; and for this reason, those who are
> superstitious will be wise to fling open their doors
> and windows so that any spirits that may have
> found their way into the house may be driven out.

Christmas came into its own as a day of merriment and ghostly wonder during Victorian times. On 19th December 1843, the publication of Charles Dickens' 'A Christmas Carol' certainly helped in sealing this reputation. It is too easy to say that Charles Dickens invented the relationship between Christmas and Ghost stories, especially when research shows that it was a tradition in many houses that after Christmas Dinner, the family would come together around the hearth to tell supernatural stories. (During these post-dinner story sessions, the "Monster of Glamis" and other tales about the castle were invented by the Bowes-Lyon family.)

Washington Irving, in his 1819 book "The Sketch Book of Geoffrey Crayon" wrote,

> I found the company seated around the fire, listening to the parson, who was deeply ensconced in a high-backed oaken chair, the work of some cunning artificer of yore, which had been brought from the library for his particular accommodation." From this venerable piece of furniture, with which his shadowy figure and dark weazen face so admirably accorded, he was dealing forth strange accounts of popular superstitions and legends of the surrounding country, with which he had become acquainted in the course of his antiquarian researches.

The Hampshire Telegraph wrote about Christmas Day stories "although the Yuletide log may burn cheerily on the hearth, the wassail bowl go merrily round, and the well-spread board resounds with shouts of revelry and mirth, yet overall there hangs a cloud of fear, a sense of mystery, which says as plain as a whisper in the ear, the place is haunted."

For hundreds of years before Dickens, the tradition of a Christmas story, or to be specific a "Winter's Tale", existed in Europe. By looking at the works of Joseph Glanvill, William Shakespeare and Christopher Marlow, there are several references to the term "Winter's Tale" being used to describe a story relating to ghosts and the macabre.

The combination of ingrained religious beliefs and the steady increase in interest in ghosts led to the boom of real and fictional ghost stories in Victorian times.

I believe it was also a time when people no longer felt threatened to discuss their experiences, for the threat of repercussion from the dead as well as the living no longer existed on the scale as it once was believed. The public's increase in sightings and more ghostly literature publishing fanned the flames of the public's appetite for the paranormal.

Based on the research I have undertaken, between 1800 and 1849, there are an impressive 24,000 mentions of ghosts in the press. However, between 1850 and 1899, there were over 161,000 mentions of ghosts – a figure unmatched in the following century. That kind of constant coverage in national and local newspapers would have kept ghosts firmly in the public's mindset, and hence why you are reading this very book over a hundred years later.

MJ Wayland
Halloween 2021

The Misty Figure

Many years ago, journalist and television presenter Willy (RWF) Poole told a story about his first season as a master of the Dartmoor Foxhounds.

On Christmas Eve, the hunt met at a pub on the edge of the moor. The landlord sniffed the air and said snow was on the way. A fox was found at Piles Wood, and soon the hounds were streaking away up the rocky valley. They ran past Erme Pits, an open cast tin mine and on to the bogs of "The Struggy" and the fog on top of the moor.

Riders started peeling off for home, and by the time Poole reached Green Hill, he was alone in the mist with the occasional cry of hounds and the first flakes of snow. He was about to turn back when a figure beckoned him to follow him. He could not make him out in what was now a blizzard, but he could see that he was a little wiry figure riding a sharp-looking, iron-grey horse. As they climbed higher, the ground got worse, and Mr Poole, who could not look into the driving snow, noticed they were on a faint path.

"The path undulated as we rode along it," wrote Mr Poole. "I know what this was – the infamous Black Lane, a man-made track across the wet green mosses, mosses which would swallow a horse. Few people rode Black Lane in good weather, certainly not in a blizzard. I had not heard the hounds for some time but was more concerned with survival, so I clung to my guide as he flitted through the murk.

At last, we emerged from the bog onto the slightly better ground around Swincombe Heads. The misty figure held up his hand, and we stopped. Sure enough, I could hear hounds coming to my left.

We held on at a trot, my horse being very tired now. Then suddenly, we dropped below the cloud into the Swincombe Valley, just in time to see the hounds catch their fox by the moor gate. I knew that I was safe now - I just had to follow the track down from the gate. My guide had been beside me, and I turned to thank him, but he waved a hand and was swallowed up in the cloud."

Later that day, Poole sat in a farmer's kitchen called John and related the eerie encounter. John unhooked a picture from the wall of a wiry little man on an iron-grey horse with a ratty tail., "That's Limpety, the gipsy huntsman; he died in a blizzard on Swincombe Heads fifty years ago on Christmas Eve."

The Flying Hearse

The spectre of a Flying Hearse is the last thing you would expect to see on Christmas Eve, or anytime, to be honest. However, in Webheath on the outskirts of Redditch, the Foxlydiate Arms Hotel claims to have an association with this strange haunting.

In 1781 Sarah Hemming purchased three houses near Foxlydiate Gate; a relative, Mr W Hemming, demolished the houses and built himself a country mansion, calling it Foxlydiate House. The story about the house is one of antiquity and seems to relate to a murder by an evil vicar.

Many years ago, there was a quarrel between the vicar and curate of nearby Studley, who was covering for the vicar of Tardebigge. On Christmas Eve, the verger of Tardebrigge died, leaving the vicar or curate of Studley having to conduct a funeral service on Boxing Day, missing the day's hunting. The vicar flew into a rage and, after a very heated argument, killed the curate. In desperation, the vicar took the curate's body, borrowed the hearse and horses, and secretly buried the curate in the grave meant for the verger. On his way back to Studley, the vicar is said to have killed Bill Attewood, a poacher, by thrusting his head into a mantrap – and so started the annual appearances of a hearse without the driver manifesting on Christmas Eve when the moon is full.

Another legend states that those who witness the hearse and horses will die within the year, yet one person lived to tell the tale when he witnessed the hearse a few miles south of Foxlydiate.

Talking to author Anne Bradford, he said, "I could hear this cart coming nearer and nearer. It was only a narrow lane, and I thought I was going to get run over... I could hear it and feel it, but although it was a bright, moonlight night, I couldn't see a thing."

The Foxlydiate Arms now stands just a few yards from A448 Bromsgrove Highway. It will be interesting to see if the hearse is seen on this modern road over time and whether the legend continues.

He Looked Right Through Me

In 1892 the houses of St George's Road, Kilburn, London, were only forty years old and known for being substantial, solid and very comfortable, far removed from what you would imagine as being a typical haunted home. And yet No 27, a terrace house with a pretty, small garden, held a terrifying secret that the family struggled to hold over eighteen months.

The house for many years had been the dwelling for various ministers who have succeeded each other every three years at Quex Road Chapel. Reverend G S Tyler and his family moved into the home in late 1892, and sightings of a 'ghost' began.

Tyler commented,

> I have never seen the apparition myself and have always been a confirmed unbeliever in spirit manifestations and so on. But the fact remains, explain it how you will, that my wife and my daughters Ada and Julie, aged respectively twenty and nineteen years, have distinctly seen a mysterious "something" which in the absence of any better way of describing it, we have called an apparition. They agree closely in their several descriptions of the figure. It is that of a person attired as a Wesleyan minister in black clothes of a clerical cut. It is a figure of average stature, with a long grey beard and keen peculiar eyes. It was my youngest daughter who first met with the apparition.

Julie Tyler was interviewed at the time by the Pall Mall Gazette; she discussed a sighting that occurred just before Christmas; she claimed, "I was standing at the corner of the stairs, and I saw what I took to be Pa. I had gone to call him to tea, and he neither answered nor moved when I called him. I thought he was playing with me and giving me the trouble to go up to him, and I ran up to push him. I pushed right

"I shall never forget his eyes – greyish blue in colour, and they seemed to look right through me."

through the figure and fell against the wall. I was dreadfully frightened, but when I told the others, they laughed at me."

Soon after, her sister Ada and mother encountered the dark figure. Ada related her own experience of the uncanny visitor.

She was alone in the house one Sunday evening and saw the figure in the doorway. She thought that a man had broken into the house at first until she realised what the figure was wearing and remembered her sister's earlier sighting.

Mrs Tyler encountered the figure while passing a small room at the end of a passage in the house. As she passed, she thought she could see Reverend Tyler standing in the room. She made her way up to the study, and that it was here, she found the real Reverend Tyler in the flesh.

Throughout the family's inhabitation of 27 St George's Road, the small room at the end of the passage was the epicentre of the haunting, with the ladies of the household refusing to venture near it alone. Miss Julie, during her interview, remarked, "It was in that room that I met the figure face to face. I shall never forget his eyes – greyish blue in colour, and they seemed to look right through me."

The story of the Tyler's haunting appeared in several newspapers, and the last mention in March 1893 seems to signal the end of the haunting itself. Soon afterwards, the road was renamed Priory Terrace, and the house numbers changed – effectively ruling out any modern investigation of this thoroughly strange haunting.

The Lone Mountain Musician

Emmitsburg, Maryland, may not be as well-known as the close by Gettysburg, but it certainly has 'history'. Named after its founder William Emmit in 1785 (previously known as 'Silver Fancy'), the town had a relatively quiet time until the Civil War. The Union army fortified the town to stop the Confederate invasion of June 1863.

Strangely on 23rd June, a mysterious fire broke out, burning half the town to the ground. While 'The Great Fire', as it was known in folklore, became the talk of the town, with many believe a Union sympathiser started the fire to stop the advancing Confederates from taking supplies. Whatever the truth, the town was spared a battle, with it taking place just 12 miles north near the Pennsylvania town of Gettysburg.

Emmitsburg sits at the bottom of the Catoctin Mountain, a part of the easternmost mountain ridge of the Blue Ridge Mountains, which in turn are a part of the Appalachian Mountain range. The mountain is probably best known for being the site of "Camp David', the mountain retreat for the Presidents of the United States.

One must wonder if the following ghost story was ever experienced by the staff or indeed the Presidents during their visits?

Professor Henry Caspar Dielman, who in the 1800s was one of the most celebrated musicians in the country, lived in Emmitsburg with his family. Henry was also the composer of the "Inauguration Marches" of four Presidents of the United States and many sacred songs. Dielman was well known locally for his love of Christmas, and before Dawn, on Christmas day, he would assemble the school orchestra and awaken his students with 'Adeste Fidelis' (O' Come All Ye Faithful).

Another tradition Henry started was playing his violin on Christmas Eve night while hidden in the woods above St Mary on the Hill, a Catoctin Mountain church.

"My grandmother, who was born on the mountain in 1858, recalled the family talking about the music that he made on the mountain on Christmas Eve," said Frances Bittle, whose family had lived in the area for nearly two hundred years.

Sadly, his son Lawrence 'Larry' Dielman, even though schooled on the flute, had no interest in classical music and began to play the popular instrument of the time, the banjo.

Instead of following in his father's footsteps, he married and opened a general store in town. Larry could often be seen sitting on his general store porch singing his own compositions for the local girls. Things took a turn in 1882 when his father died. Filled with regret, and now divorced, he decided to continue his Father's Christmas Eve tradition and played at his father's graveside on the mountain, near to where his father would hide in the woods.

That Christmas in 1883, Larry walked to his father's grave near the Grotto of Our Lady of Lourdes. As he stood by the harshly carved gravestone, he lifted the flute to his lips for the first time. Townfolks recalled hearing the strains of the melody to "When Glory Lit the Midnight Air," a composure of Larry's recently deceased father.

"His tribute, with carols on the flute his father played to parental memory on Christmas morning, is perhaps the prettiest ever paid a parent by a son," wrote the Frederick Evening Post on December 24th 1912.

Upon one of these occasions, it had snowed throughout the night, and Christmas morning, the mountain was picturesquely cloaked in white. Through the surrounding valleys, oil lamps flickered in the dark as they shone from windows. All was quiet as the country children listened and watched for some trace of good St Nicholas' visit to their homes in the starlight. Suddenly the stillness of the crisp winter morning was broken by the sweet notes of a flute coming from the direction of the mountains. The first suggestion was one of weirdness, which, however, was soon

dispelled as the sacred refrains of 'Adeste Fidelis'
were heard.

From 1884 until 1923, for 39 years, Larry made the journey, no matter
the weather, to the grave high up on the mountain, and for hours on
that Christmas Eve would play his father's favourite Christmas songs.

Larry, or the lone mountain musician, became a minor celebrity with
his fame being known around the land. Journalists came to
Emmitsburg to interview him and why he continued the tradition.

Larry is a picturesque son of the mountains, as
rugged as the hills he has always called home and
possesses all the vigour that a life of freedom can
endow. He is six feet of brawn, with an eye as alert
as ever." Larry probably would have laughed at
his description, but when the journalist asked him
why he continued his tribute, he was resolute,
"After my father passed away, I still had the flute
which he had presented to me, so now for these
many years I have taken it up the mountain, and
there we meet again, wherein spirit he may join me
in the Christmas carols.

Just a few years after this interview, Larry passed away. But this isn't
the end of the story, because Larry did not stop his touching tribute to
his father even in death. In 1967, 45 years after his death, newspapers
reported that Larry could still be heard on Christmas Eve.

Some say the tunes were mournful, a memento to
the death of his musician father and to the love
Larry never rekindled with the wife who left him.
While others maintain they have heard music
though solemn at times, was a jubilant start to
Christmas Day.

In the 1960s and 70s, several townspeople still remembered the old
man playing 'Silent Night' on his flute and then entering St Anthony's
Church wrapped in a shawl to observe the midnight services.

One witness clearly remembered the sound of the music after Larry's death. "You've got to understand ... I was only a boy at the time, but oh sure, I heard the music year after year," said Eugene Warthen in a 1977 interview with The Evening Sun.

"I remember the sounds of Christmas night, the sleigh bells, the laughter of people bundled up for the cold weather on the sleighs and the howling of the dogs at the flute music," he said.

It was Christmas Eve, 1922, when Larry last played the flute. According to legend, he began his normal piping on the mountain, faltered, and then the music ceased altogether. By the time townsfolk arrived at the cemetery on the hill, Larry was unconscious and had died in the spring. He was buried in a plot next to his father.

Over the years, there have been numerous reports of the flute echoing down the mountainside. Families would make a special trip to sit on the hillside on Christmas Eve to hear the spectral music while others would stay in the safety of their homes listening intently.

Some years Larry could be heard alone, sometimes a laugh could be heard, and sometimes, townsfolk reported they could hear a flute and a violin.

Larry and Henry, Son and Father were once again, reunited.

The Ghost of Constable Tower

London has a Christmas ghost. Moreover, it is the
ghost of a lady; and it has revisited the glimpses of
the moon within the precincts of that grey and
time-worn centre of London's tragedy and
London's romance, The Tower.

Manchester Times - 28th December 1900

The Tower of London is famed for its ghosts. For centuries, there have
been tales of phantom footsteps, manifestations, and omens within its
walls, but I will discuss its only Christmas haunting for this book.

On Christmas Eve, 1900, a poor officer who lived in the Constable's
Tower within the Tower of London, heard a long, drawn-out wail
coming from the top of the tower. Since it was late, around 9:00 pm,
he decided to investigate in case someone was breaking into the
castle. When he reached the stairs, he once again the wail sounded but
this time, closer.

Suddenly he heard a distinct light footstep receding behind the arras (a
wall hanging or tapestry) in one of the rooms down the corridor. In
total, three times, a sad, low, wailing cry trembled through the tower,
and each time the soft footfall was heard retreating behind the arras.

The officer searched the whole tower several times, but nothing could
be found. Days later, he met with Captain Jupp, a former guard at
Constable Tower, and he confirmed that there had been similar strange
activity reported by previous officers based there. Interestingly,
Captain Jupp also claimed that several Chelsea Pensioners (retired ex-
military) witnessed the spectre of a middle-aged gentleman of long ago
with a peaked hat, pointed beard, cloak, and sword over Christmas.

The ghost was seen walking with a dejected gait, his head sunk low and
his hand to his chin; he was seen near the state apartments set aside as
the governor's residence. In the state apartments, there have been
rumours and conjecture that it is haunted and said to have secret
passages running to and from the precinct.

The Clanking Ghost

East Barnet and South Mimms in North London are two suburbs known for being leafy, calm and comfortable, yet are classed as 'haunted lands' by many researchers. Within this relatively small area, there are hundreds of reports of ghosts and paranormal activity.

A thousand years ago, these 'haunted lands' were heavily wooded and were a part of a larger area, including Chipping or High Barnet - where the Battle of Barnet took place. The Abbot of St Albans once owned most of this land, but in his resistance to William the Conqueror, he lost the southern part of his lands to the Bishop of London.

One of the knights who fought alongside William the Conqueror at Hastings was Geoffrey de Mandeville from Dieppe in France. After the battle, he was given large swathes of land across Essex, Middlesex and adjoining counties. He became one of ten knights who were the highest ranking in England.

However, fortunes changed with his son William. In 1100 William was the Constable of the Tower of London; unfortunately, one of his prisoners, Ranulf Flambard, escaped. This had great repercussions for the de Mandevilles and William. As punishment, King Henry I confiscated William's three richest estates, Barnet included.

William's son Geoffrey set about to recover the family's fortunes through manipulation and political manoeuvring. By 1141 it began to pay off, and Sir Geoffrey was the premier baron of England. He was known for his ruthlessness and created many powerful enemies, one of which became the King. Geoffrey misplayed the political game just once and paid for it dearly. During the battles between Stephen and Matilda, Geoffrey changed sides several times depending on who was in the most powerful position at the time. This was a battle for the crown, so Geoffrey had to choose well. Sadly, like many barons of the time, he picked Matilda. In 1143 after Stephen's release from prison and coronation, the King arrested the earl. Threatened with execution, Geoffrey surrendered his castles and estates to King Stephen and in reaction, he launched a rebellion.

For over a year, Sir Geoffrey operated as a rebel, mainly in the fen country. Eventually, he was besieged by King Stephen, meeting a bloody death in September 1144. Because he was excommunicated, his body was denied burial by all churches except one. His corpse was wrapped in lead and taken to the Templar Church in London, where his effigy can still be seen today.

Why Geoffrey haunts East Barnet's Oak Hill Park and only appears at Christmas time. No one knows for sure; there are dozens of witnesses to the ghost of a cloaked knight.

In 1926, Geoffrey's "clanking ghost" hit the headlines after a night watchman's experience was read out as part of the East Barnet district councillors' minutes. The night watchman in question had been working in Oak Hill Park during the recent road workings. A week before Christmas, he witnessed a figure enveloped in a long military cloak near a building that stands in the park. The nightwatchman observed the ghost long enough to realise that the cloak was see-through and the figure within was a skeleton. The councillors put forward the motion that the night watchman should have an increased wage due to the issues he was experiencing! Another watchman was asked to relieve the former watchman's shift but began to shake like a leaf and refused to take over.

Interestingly the building where the night watchman had his experience was previously a part of the East Barnet workhouse founded in the early 1700s. Known as the "The Shanty", the building had a reputation for many years as being haunted both by the "clanking ghost" and mistreated children who were punished by being locked in the cellars below. The children's ghosts haunt the building after some were lost in the vast underground passages, never to be seen again. At the time of the roadworks in 1926, many people expected the workmen involved to bring to light long-hidden secrets connected with the old workhouse.

Several journalists took to ghost hunting in the park after the newspaper reports of the night watchman's encounter with Sir Geoffrey. A Western Times journalist wrote,

> Even the prospect of handsome photographs in
> the illustrated papers failed to tempt shy Geoffrey
> into the upper air today.... Every effort to trace
> him since the debate with a view to ascertaining
> whether he was a sufficiently disagreeable person
> to warrant extra payment to the night watchman
> had proved vain. Nevertheless, residents believe
> Geoffrey is lurking about somewhere in the
> neighbourhood.

Two years later, great expectations had built for Geoffrey's return at Christmas, and he held his promise; on Christmas Eve, he appeared.

> A few minutes before midnight near the old parish
> church at East Barnet, I saw in the distance a
> vague figure dressed in a heavy cloak, moving
> towards me from the direction of the Farm Home.
> I stood still and waited for this to approach, but
> suddenly it seemed to pass through a wall and
> disappear in the fields in the direction of Trent
> Barnet. As I waited and listened, I distinctly heard
> sounds like the clanking of spurs but saw nothing
> more of the strange figure.

The witness, not named in the report, was allegedly part of a ghost hunt organised by the East Barnet Research Society. The group organised members to be posted each night in different parts of the park to observe any ghostly activity.

When asked if the society would use force to rid the park of the ghost, they replied, "the purpose of the Research Society is to get into communication with the ghost quietly and try, if possible; to find out why Sir Geoffrey's spirit remains earthbound."

A year later, the East Barnet Research Society was reported to be undertaking an even larger ghost hunt of Barnet and South Mimms, due to the reports of Rev. Allen Hay, a vicar. He had an experience with a supernatural presence in his bedroom and a relative of his met the ghost of an Elizabethan woman in the village hall. Even South

Mimms church at the time was alleged to be haunted by a clergyman dressed in white robes walking from the chancel and through a wall.

Due to the upsurge of sightings of Sir Geoffrey and other ghosts in the area at Christmas, the society decided to ban the press and other paranormal investigators.

The police were asked to regulate the queues of thousands of visitors armed with cameras and flash lamps to see Sir Geoffrey. Leading up to the ghost hunt, more paranormal activity was reported, including the dogs in the neighbourhood becoming very restless at nightfall and a woman reporting the sound of muffled drums coming from the park over two successive nights.

With the ghost hunt cloaked in secrecy, we do not know if Geoffrey once again made his return that night, but in 1932 the park had such a reputation that a local Justice of the Peace described Church Hill Road, which runs by the park, as "The Ghost's Promenade".

Another ghost hunt took place at Christmas 1933, and a reporter wrote,

> I, as with many others, gathered in the old village
> to await the arrival of the ghostly visitor. The night
> was cold and cloudy. There was a woodland copse
> in the background. As we stood, staring, there was
> a sudden break in the clouds, and there could be
> seen clearly a figure in armour – Sir Geoffrey de
> Mandeville.

Jack Hallam, in his book "Ghosts of London", claims that the first vigil after World War II brought nearly four hundred ghost hunters from all parts of London, sadly the only thing they saw that night was the mist swirl through the trees and along the gully known as Pym's Brook.

East Barnet seems to be one of Britain's most haunted, if not active locations, with the local press claiming, "Headless hounds, decapitated bodies, spectres in the trees - the list of ghostly experiences at Oak Hill Park in East Barnet seems to go on and on."

The Squire's Ghost

Many Yuletide ghost stories relate to hunting, probably a distant remnant of a tradition lost in time. One such ghost story is from the pretty North Devon village of Combe Martin. Situated in a narrow valley that runs to the sea, Combe Martin is principally a single street running two miles long.

Combe Martin is the place if tradition has stuck around anywhere in Devon, hidden away in the ginnels and alleyways. The town has several very old, traditional events, from 'The Hunting of the Earl of Rone', which features a rare 'hobby horse' from folklore tradition to the Strawberry Fayre in June. To the outsider, these activities seem strange and bizarre, if not otherworldly, and that indeed was the purpose.

The village is said to have three ghosts, but the most celebrated is that of its Christmas Ghost, Squire Usticke. Many a warning was heeded when it was told that if you walked the streets of Combe Martin after midnight on Christmas Eve, then you would encounter the spectre of the Squire, the master of the old manor house next to near the village's church.

When Squire Usticke died, preparations were made for a grand funeral, and a great gathering of the relations, neighbours and local gentry took place at the mansion.

All his servants, except one, were ordered to join the funeral procession, it being the Devonian custom to assess the reputation of a dead person by the numbers who escorted him to his grave, but when a serving maid also stayed behind, she was in for a fright.

Even in 1867, many remembered the maid's name, Jane Bullock. Jane stayed at the mansion to cook the 'funeral baked meats' for the mourners on their return.

Whether Jane was worn out with her chores or overwhelmed with grief, knowing she would be unsupervised for a few hours, she sat down for a rest in her late master's favourite chair. Scarcely had she sat in the chair when her master's form appeared before her and, in a stern and booming voice, told her to immediately, "Get out of that, and go and mind your work."

Not long after, the funeral party returned after depositing their poor friend in his family vault. A small group entered the sitting room where Jane lies prosaic on the floor after the terror of seeing her very dead Master. However, the group began to shout in horror and alarm; sitting in his chair was the Squire himself, smoking his pipe by his fireside. How the rest of the funeral party continued after the Squire's appearance is unknown, but in 1847, Jane Bullock's family still told the story well over a hundred years later.

The Squire still wanders his old mansion, smoking his pipe if you fancy a trip to North Devon. However, it is said that just after midnight on Christmas Eve, he likes to wander down the dark lane that still goes by his name "Usticke Lane" and into the village of Combe Martin.

Dare you meet the Squire?

A Boy and His Horse

Coton Hall near Alveley, Bridgnorth, with its links with the infamous Lee family, is an idyllic historic house with ties to American and British history. The family originally named "de la Lee" of Norman descent have lived on the site of Coton Hall since the 1300s.

The present Hall was built in the early 1800s for Harry Lee; interestingly, the previous Hall was the building Robert E. Lee's ancestors left for America in the 1600s. Originally a trading family, soon the Lee family forged a new life. Two of them, Richard Henry and Francis Lightfoot Lee, were the only brothers to sign the Declaration of Independence. General Robert E. Lee's father was 'Light Horse Harry' Lee, a famous soldier of the Revolutionary War, where he was known for his courage in fighting the British.

Little remains of the house of Robert E Lee's ancestors, but in its ground remains a 13th Century chapel. The cellar is two storeys deep underneath the present house and includes a tunnel said to stretch to Alveley village two miles away!

And it is one of the Lee family that haunts the Hall and its grounds on Christmas Eve. A son was to receive a beautiful white horse for Christmas from his parents. Unfortunately, the son was very impatient and received it beforehand, thundering off across Coton Hall's grounds.

No one knows for sure what happened, but as he was riding around the park, he went into some trees where it is believed he caught his neck on a branch, fell from the horse, and died of a broken neck.

For countless years locals believed that at midnight on Christmas Eve, you could witness the ghost of the boy on the white horse.

On Christmas Eve 1978, Les Hunt was walking home with a girl from the village hall's annual dance. As he reached the edge of the park, he saw a gate open by itself. Rather startled, he continued walking, and a few moments later, it closed again by unseen forces! He went back to the gate and searched the area, but nothing could explain how such a heavy gate could open and close on its own. Maybe Hunt encountered the ghost boy without realising it?

Colonel Sidley's Christmas Ride

There are many tales of ghosts and spirits in Norfolk's historic houses and indeed its countryside. Across Britain, there are numerous tales of a ghostly 'wild hunt' setting out on Christmas Eve, searching the countryside for poor souls to take. This following story could be classed as one such wild hunt story but with one resounding difference – it is a story based on fact.

This story concerns Colonel Sidley and his activities at Ranworth Hall, Norfolk, on Christmas Eve 1770. Some people still swear that the galloping hooves of his great mare, Black Jezebel, can be heard thundering across the windswept countryside on Christmas Eve. Others reckon that they have heard the mare plunge into the water of the nearby broad.

Colonel Sidley was a wild man with a passion for wine, women, and hunting. The people of Ranworth feared him for being cruel and bitter in his dealings with them; he had the reputation of being possessed with a devil, or even being the devil himself. His startling appearance supported these beliefs, for he always wore dark, sombre clothes, his hair was jet black, and his dark eyes glinted evilly. He remained booted and spurred at all times, ready to ride Black Jezebel at a moment's notice, always at the gallop.

He would call out his hounds at any time of the day, then ride the huge black mare like a demon. Woe betide anyone who got in his way or tried to interfere with his sport, small wonder the country folk of Ranworth instinctively sought cover at the sound of the approach of this galloping fiend.

Life at Ranworth Hall was equally hectic. Often lights from every window blazed out long into the night. On these occasions, the sounds of drunken songs, laughter, shrieks, and screams echoed across the surrounding countryside.

Characteristically, Colonel Sidley sent invitations to half the local gentry and a group of local blades from Norwich to ride to hounds with him on the stroke of midnight on Christmas Eve, 1770. The guests arrived to find the colonel ready to ride, but first, he insisted on them finishing a bowl of punch.

By the time midnight approached, few of the men were sober, and a whoop of enthusiasm broke out as Colonel Sidley rose to his feet, brandished his riding crop and urged the company to finish their drinks, then follow him to the stables. Before he reached the main door, a loud bang was heard upon it. Suddenly it flew open, and a solitary figure in a voluminous black cloak filled the doorway. The stranger wore a large black hat that concealed his features. In a harsh commanding voice, he invited Colonel Sidley to ride with him. He also pointed to other members of the company. Flushed with drinking, the men went for their horses, and the hounds burst from their kennels. A servant came forward with the colonel's cloak, but the stranger brushed him aside, saying, "he will need no cloak this night."

At the sight of the stranger, the hounds suddenly turned tail and fled howling. The sky had become heavily overcast, and peals of thunder rent the air. Halted by these strange signs, the men watched a flash of lightning zigzag across the sky.

By this eerie light, they saw their host gallop off with the stranger in the direction of Ranworth Broad. Suddenly an agonised shriek pierced out above the storm, followed by a great splash of water, then a chilling momentary silence before a bell began to toll softly.

Guests and servants fled in all directions, leaving the hall shining out like a beacon in the surrounding blackness, but Colonel Sidley did not return.

The following morning his solicitor came from Norwich. He announced that he had received an urgent summons. He turned deathly white when told of the nature of the colonel's departure. He then collected all the dead man's papers and burnt the lot.

It was never discovered who tolled the bell or who summoned the solicitor. Still, because of these mysterious happenings and the riding of the ghostly horses on Christmas Eve, Ranworth Hall remained empty for a long time. In 1985 it was finally demolished, leaving only its old porch as a reminder of its terrible history.

Today, in summer, Ranworth is a popular holiday village thronged with holidaymakers from the Norfolk Broads. In winter, however, it is lonely and deserted, and on Christmas Eve, the past can be resurrected by the prospect of Colonel Sidley riding Black Jezebel again.

Tragedy At Calverley Hall

Yorkshire has its fair share of ghosts that like to appear at Christmas, but one story has drifted into legend and become known for its romance and murder.

In the picturesque hills between Leeds and Bradford sits the quiet, sleepy village of Calverley, and in this village is a very haunted manor.

Calverley Hall adjoins a burial ground whose ancient yew trees cast long, haunting shadows across its lawns. The Hall was once the residence of Walter Calverley and generations of Calverleys.

The Hall has now been split into several dwellings, yet the part where a dastardly deed took place stands in a ruinous state. The pedigree of the ancient Calverley family has been traced back to the 1400s, and the Hall was a noted place of great importance and mediaeval comfort.

Walter Calverley was just seventeen when his father died, and the estate was placed in the hands of his mother and great uncle William until Walter reached manhood at twenty-one years.

In Summer 1599, Walter married Phillipa Brooke, and this was a good marriage indeed for the Calverleys. Phillipa was part of London's high society, and her family was involved in the royal circle. In fact, Phillipa's mother was directly related to Sir Robert Cecil, 1st Earl of Salisbury, the spymaster of King James I. The marriage surprised many as the couple were from such different social backgrounds.

Within a year, the marriage ran into difficulties and famously, Phillipa's mother, Lady Brooke, wrote to Sir Robert, "one Mr Calverley her Maiesties Warde who hath married my daughter, an unstayed younge man". By 'unstayed', she presumably meant 'unstable' or 'unbalanced' of the mind.

In 1600 Walter was reported to be in prison due to debts and dangerously ill; Lady Brooke once again sought Sir Robert's help to somehow help her daughter be removed from her husband. However,

Walter did not die, and following his release from prison, Walter and Phillipa had their first child, William, in early 1601. Sadly, it was also the year that Walter had to sell off major plots of land around Calverley, Pudsey and the East Riding.

Two more children were born (Walter and Henry), and the family became more unsettled due to financial worries and the pull to London from Phillipa. She was used to living in style; her residence in London was Durham House, the former property of Queen Elizabeth. No matter how comfortable, Calverley Hall was no match for the social circles and style of London.

What happened next has been covered many times by many writers, and at one time, it was believed that even William Shakespeare had written a version, but here is the tale as factually known.

On 23rd April 1605, on hearing that a relative had been arrested for a debt that he was responsible, Walter went out of the house to get drunk. Returning in a drunken frenzy later than day, he rushed into the house; he snatched up one and then another of his children and plunged his dagger into them both and threw them on the floor.

He then tried to take Phillipa's life, but the steel in her corset saved her life. Walter believing her to be dead, left the hall hurriedly, giving the intent to his servants that he was riding to kill his youngest son, Henry, "a brat at nurse".

The servant called for help, and the villagers overpowered Walter and threw him off his horse. Walter was brought to trial at York, but he refused to plead, knowing that doing so would mean his estate's forfeiture to the crown, and his son would receive nothing. Instead of the usual hanging as punishment for his crimes, Walter was sentenced to be pressed to death at York Castle.

Tradition or local legend says that an old servant was with him when they put stones on his chest to crush him to death. The criminal begged for mercy from his servant. The servant complied with his request and was promptly hanged for his trouble. Walter was believed to have been buried at St Mary's Castlegate, York but I cannot find any proof of his burial, strangely. Again, local tradition states that he was secretly buried at Calverley alongside sixteen generations of the Calverleys. Little wonder that Calverley Hall and its surroundings are regarded as haunted grounds after such a dire tragedy.

Walter has returned as a spectral horseman seen galloping about the district on a headless horse at night, sometimes being chased by ghostly villagers.

The ghostly horseman became so troublesome to the village in the mid-1700s that the Vicar of Calverley church undertook the task of 'laying the ghost', and for a hundred years, it seemed a success.

In 1847, Rev. Richard Burdsall, having preached in the village, stayed at the Hall. It was early January, and he retired to bed at midnight. Several minutes later, he claimed to have experienced, "I had not been asleep long before I thought something crept up to my breast, pressing me much. I was greatly agitated and struggled hard to awake."

Suddenly the bed moved, and Richard was thrown to the floor. He thanked God and returned to the bed, where he was again thrown on the floor fifteen minutes later.

> I was thrown off the bed a third time. After this, I
> once more crept under the bed to ascertain
> whether all the cords were fast…and found all
> (was) right. I now put on my clothes, not
> attempting to lie down anymore.

For six hours, Richard kept vigil without awakening the household in his account of his experience he wrote, "I longed to see the light of the morning, and had I been immured in a dungeon and heavily fettered in irons, I could not have been more desirous of my liberty than I was for the return of the morning."

Three years later, a man named Parson Greenwood had a similar experience, and the villagers began to speak of ghosts in the churchyard. It became a local tradition that some of the villagers held a vigil at Christmas to look for the ghost of Walter Calverley, while others just played tricks.

The ghost became the focus for the school children in the area who decided to raise Walter from the grave. A writer of one article describes how the children would meet in the churchyard of Calverley and then "put their hats and caps down on the ground, in a pyramidical form. Then taking hold of each other's hands, they formed a 'magic circle' holding firmly together and making use of an old refrain –

Old Calverley, Old Calverley, I have thee by the
ears,

I'll cut thee into collops, unless thee appear

Some of the more venturesome boys had to go round to each of the church doors and whistle aloud through the keyhole, repeating the magical couplet while their comrades in the circle were chanting."

This happened on many occasions, but only once did a "pale and ghostly figure" appear. It came forward out of the church sending the boys into different directions, fearful to avoid the ghost's grasp.

In 1871, according to a report published thirteen years later, the bell at Calverley church began tolling at 1:00am on a January morning; when curious villagers went to investigate, the tolling stopped the moment they entered the church. The incident was blamed on Walter Calverley's ghost.

On the 18th December 1904, the ghost of Calverley was spotted by a man from nearby Horsforth. The man was passing the church when he heard 'weird sounds' coming from the direction of the graveyard. Suddenly there was a large flash, and a phantom-like form floated before the astonished man. Within a few seconds, the apparition disappeared, leaving the man in a quiet state of bewilderment. The next day the man told a friend of his sighting who knew of the old legend; the man believed he witnessed Walter Calverley.

Since the modernisation of Calverley village and its Old Hall, the ghost seems far less active. Recently the Landmark Trust opened one of the wings of the Hall for accommodation for those who may wish to be thrown out of bed.

But what happened to Phillipa and Henry Calverley, you may ask? Phillipa remarried four years after her husband's execution. She had three children in her second marriage (all girls) and died in 1613. The 'brat at nurse', Henry, lived to have major financial problems of his own, dying in January 1652. His eldest son, Walter, took some sound advice and married a rich girl, Julia Blackett and became Sir Walter Calverley, 1st Baronet.

Christmas Tricks

The Welsh village of Llandoga, between Chepstow and Monmouth, came to the attention of national newspapers due to a poltergeist that came active at the Christmas of 1823.

> The windows shake, the drawers crack, each thinks
> that Nick's behind his back.

So wrote a correspondent to the Bristol Mercury investigating William Edwards, a former preacher whose haunted house was classed as being in the league as the notable haunting of the time known as "Scratching Fanny", the Cock Lane Ghost – another poltergeist story.

It was reported that an invisible spirit had made Edwards and his family's life utter hell. It became so violent that it demolished earthenware and broke glasses. Poor William believed the poltergeist to be living in his house. He relocated to another location in the village only for the 'crockery destroying demon' to pursue him to the new home. Then, the poltergeist seems to have found this move disagreeable and began kicking furniture down the stairs and generally causing damage and mayhem around William Edwards.

A correspondent visiting Llandoga interviewed the locals and concluded that what was happening was real, although the villagers had various ideas on what was really happening. Mr Edwards was reported to believe he was 'buffeting Satan, on his determination to become a new man'.

Another villager claimed that Edwards once promised to meet a ghost or sprite to try and find hidden treasure with it but had forgotten the appointment! Sadly, the Llandoga poltergeist disappears from history, and we never discover the truth behind the poltergeist or if indeed it ever stopped haunting poor William Edwards.

Taddington Hall's Christmas Ghosts

Situated in the scenic Derbyshire countryside Taddington Hall is one of the lesser-known stately homes, mainly because it has remained a private residence for over three hundred years.

Of course, the Hall has ghosts, or at least Christmas ghosts.

The first reported ghost came from the winter of 1947 and was told by Bill Furniss, a local farmer. Furniss had been called to the Hall to deal with a sick mare, whom he moved from the snowy fields to the warmth of the Hall's stables. Several times the mare bolted from the stables and acted as if she was unnerved. Furniss carried on struggling, and once again, she bolted. Suddenly he realised he had a helper, "Whoa" called a man's voice from the entrance. "Whoa!" Furniss went to retrieve the mare, and when he finally got to the door, he realised there was no sign of any man and no footprints in the snow.

The next day Bill talked to the owner of Taddington Hall, Lt-Col Smalley, who related the story of a terrible murder that took place in the stables.

A long time ago, two brothers ran a small hessian factory in the stables, and everything seemed to be going well, but then they began to quarrel.

One day Issac was found in the cellar with his throat cut, murdered by his brother. Since then, Issac has haunted the Hall and its stables, and Smalley believed Furniss had encountered him.

Poor murdered Issac is one ghost of Taddington Hall who appears at Christmas and on winter nights. Another is that of a previous owner who returning from Bakewell market worse for drink died at the bottom of Bakewell Hill. His ghost reputedly haunts the hall at dusk on Mondays and especially on Christmas Eve.

The Monks of Long Drax

Now sitting in the shadow of one of England's largest power stations, at one time, the riverside, sprawling hamlet of Long Drax was home to one of the earliest religious settlements in the British Isles.

These settlements of religious communities housed monks, priests (Canons) and lay-brothers (commoners who worked on the Abbey lands but followed the discipline).

Significant buried remains of the Drax Priory have been discovered across Long Drax but mainly on the land partly occupied by Drax Abbey Farm.

Founded in the 1130s, Drax Priory was founded by William Paynel on the advice of the Archbishop of York. The Canons dedicated the priory to St Nicholas (Santa Claus), and William also gave a mill, a parish church and other land to the St Augustines.

Within a couple hundred years, the Priory began to struggle; the nearby River Ouse is a tidal river that often floods. Not only that, but the Priory was frequently invaded by the Scots – and other enemies.

By 1535, during the Dissolution of the Monasteries, there were only 10 canons and 29 servants and boys, with the priory valued at just over 92 pounds.

With a relatively short inhabitancy, why is the village so haunted by the Monks?

Christmas 1922 saw a blaze of publicity when the Clark family reported their 'haunted cupboard'. Situated over half a mile away from the Drax Priory ruins, Baxter Hall Farm became the scene of an intense, if not short, Christmas haunting.

The Pall Mall Gazette reported,

Various descriptions of its appearance are given,
but it is generally agreed that it takes the form of a
tall and restless shade, doubtless revisiting the
scene of its former trials

Mrs Ernest Clark told reporters how she and her elder children had seen a dark shadowy form in their bedroom. One of the witnesses, Annie, who was described as a "bright, intelligent" girl of sixteen, told how she had seen the figure emerge from the cupboard, walk around her bed before vanishing through the wall.

When quizzed by the journalists if she saw a shadow from the moon, Annie replied that "if it was a shadow cast by the moon, it would not have travelled around the room."

Backing this story was another witness, 'Signalman Taylor' who also saw a dark figure close to Baxter Hall Farm around two o'clock in the morning as he was passing to go to work.

He turned his flash lamp in its direction, where it promptly vanished.

Ghostly Monks March

While many newspapers briefly printed the initial sighting, the Daily Mirror decided to research the story for whatever reason. After discussing the matter with villagers of Long Drax, the journalist uncovered the story of an 'impassable tunnel'.

> During excavations some years ago, this (a tunnel) was discovered, and it is said each time the search party reached a certain point in the tunnel, the candles they carried were blown out. This occurred more than once, rumour alleges, and the party gave up exploring the passage.

It was alleged that Drax Priory Farm and Baxter Old Hall were linked by this tunnel, even though there is half a mile between them both. To add further strangeness to the story, the locals claimed that Long Drax was haunted by a 'man without a head, a black figure flapping bat-like wings and a man hanging from a gallows and medieval women.'

The Yorkshire Post also wrote about the traditions of the Christmas hauntings,

> For a good many years ghosts have been "in the air in Drax". At one time, the ghosts of the monks of Abbey used to come at Christmas time at intervals and parade a long avenue of trees in the neighbourhood.

A Journalist Investigates

> Miss Clarke, who lives at the farm, is certain that she saw a spectral figure stalk around her bedroom on three nights in succession. Others talk of shadowy women, winged creatures and headless women.

A special correspondent was dispatched to Baxter Old Hall a few days after the initial story and delivered a very unusual and condescending report.

> Last night when the wind was whining down the dark lanes, and the bats were in the belfry of the village church, it seemed possible to believe anything – even the story of a local raconteur, who says he has seen fifty spectres marching in columns of four towards Drax Priory.

> The whole district is haunted, transparent owls hoot at the children, medieval women laugh in the faces of old men and headless spectres lounge about the hedgerows in their nightshirts.

> If I were more familiar with the Yorkshire dialect, there is doubt that I should be able to recount many more happenings. Unfortunately, I was unable to understand a word he said though I gathered from his manner they were extremely funny ghost stories.

The journalist goes to describe his night of ghost hunting, spending several hours in the Baxter Hall Farm waiting for the monk to appear, but heard and saw nothing. When he ventured outside, he claimed to have fallen in a ditch.

Disappointingly this is the last report of the Clarke Family's experiences at the Old Hall. Still, if we review the initial sightings, there were three members of the family who saw the initial ghost, the signalman and the 'local raconteur' – plus other villagers. While the journalist tried to downplay the stories of the area, there is no doubt that there is an aspect of truth to the sightings.

The Mysterious Hole in The Cellar

On the outskirts of the Yorkshire city of Sheffield, Dronfield is an ancient town sandwiched between Sheffield and the Peak District. The name Dronfield means 'land infested with drones' (male bees), a very strange name indeed! Interestingly the town was featured in the Domesday Book of 1086, but its history dates to the Bronze age and possibly even further.

Christmas 1903 didn't go well for a young couple who went to live in Dronfield. While the house is not named, it was said to have had a 'mysterious hole' in its cellar. Dark, deep and uncovered; apparently, it was an ancient well that the house had been built on top.

For a while, the couple lived in wedded bliss, and just before Christmas, something horrifying took place. The couple was looking after two young girls, daughters of friends and took them around Dronfield for the day, and later that night, the girls slept at the house. The young couple had not fitted all their rooms with beds, so the young husband slept on the sofa downstairs (the room above the cellar), and the wife and children slept upstairs.

In the darkest hour of the night, the young wife awoke.

At the same time, unknown to her, her husband was awoken at the same time. Footsteps could be clearly heard on the stairs, slowly they approached the room. The wife could hardly breathe in terror. She pulled her blankets closer but still stared at the door.

The steps came nearer, passed her room and entered another bedroom.

Relaxed, thinking it must be her husband fetching another blanket, she listened as the footsteps returned from the room and went downstairs.

At the same time, the husband had thought he heard his wife wandering around, maybe fetching something from the kitchen for the children. The next morning, the couple discovered that neither had been walking around in the middle of the night.

This was the first experience they had of the 'Dronfield ghost', and both believed that they had heard the footsteps of some restless spirit, maybe a former occupant. Either way, the footsteps signalled the beginning of a terrifying series of experiences.

The focus seemed to be the room above the cellar, in a particular corner. Late at night, mysterious knockings or slow, muffled bangs could be heard as if someone was in the wall, patiently, and persistently trying to hammer their way out.

The sounds would sometimes increase in volume, but are always slow and consistent. They continued night after night, and the young couple could not find any source inside or outside the house. Terrified, the couple took to sleeping with the oil lamps burning, believing somehow, this would provide protection against the ghostly lodger.

A few nights before Christmas Day, the wife awoke in the night realising the oil lamp had been turned off, and the bedroom was in pitch blackness.

She tried to scream, but the fear held her tight; she could tell the ghost was now in the bedroom. She endured the uncertainty and suspense as long as she could and, in desperation, sprung out of bed, grabbed the matches and struck a light. It was as she feared.

As the feeble light illuminated the room, she looked around and there looking at her full in the face and pointing to her, was the ghost.

A hideous sight slinking in the corner of the room, she saw a skeleton with deep dark eye sockets but seemingly full of life. She was held in speechless terror, frozen to the spot just a few feet from her sleeping husband.

The match began to burn itself down, and as it did, the apparition silently but purposely turned to the door and disappeared as the darkness enveloped the room.

The wife lurched to the bed, grabbing her husband, who woke abruptly and lit the gas light in the room. The ghost had gone.

The couple left the house in the middle of the night, the harrowing experience was enough to force them to leave, and they returned to Sheffield.

There is no explanation of why the experiences happened, but the trigger seems to be when the friend's daughters came to stay. Like the stories of the Enfield and Battersea Poltergeists, the story seems centred on young females. Since we don't know the age of the young wife, was she somehow key to the activity?

The newspapers of the day believed the well was somehow related to the hauntings,

> Why the house had been built over an old well, or why the well had never been filled in, and why the hole was always left uncovered we cannot say. We do not suggest the ghost or ghosts refused to allow the well to be covered, and that as often as covers were placed on it, they immediately disappeared, leaving not a trace behind.

She Waits By The Bridge

On the outskirts of Blackburn is a seven-hundred-year-old country manor recently converted to a modern hotel with an indoor pool, fitness centre and spa, yet still kept its ghost.

Dunkenhalgh Hall appears in history around the late 1200s. There likely stood a small mediaeval manor house until 1332, when it became the property of the Rishton family, who held it for two hundred and fifty years.

The Talbot and de Rishton families were major landowners in the area, and they were in continuous dispute over Waddington Hall, Holt Hall, and Cowhill. These property disputes came to ahead in 1581 when Sir Thomas Talbot sold his lands, including Dunkenhalgh, to Thomas Walmsley, a catholic. Thomas wanted to leave his mark, and he rebuilt Dunkenhalgh Hall and created a catholic chapel on its grounds.

Dunkenhalgh luckily missed any military damage caused by battle during the Civil War of 1640 - 1652. However, it did require £10,000 of repairs due to the parliamentarians who were based there during that time and seemed to have a jolly rollicking time!

Around 1742, Dunkenhalgh and its estate passed into the hands of the Petre family, who would hold the house for two hundred years until 1947. Strangely it is from the relatively quiet times of the Petre family that a ghost is said to haunt the Hall.

It was a local tradition that no one should pass by the Hall at midnight on Christmas Eve, as it was thought that a ghost (or boggart as they were called) would appear in the form of a young woman dressed in a white sheet. She could be seen walking from the house, along the trees, and to the site of an old bridge and then disappears.

As with many ghost stories, the origin of the haunting has no fixed date but is set when the Petre family were at their greatest strengths. A young French lady called Lucette was the children's governess, and she was in love with a young officer. The officer used Lucette and never intended to marry her, always promising that they would be married someday. One day Lucette confronted the officer, for she was now pregnant and demanded that he marry her so that she could have the child with no shame. The officer was furious and claimed she had been unfaithful, leaving her at Dunkenhalgh.

Lucette was in a predicament; she could not stay at the house as an unmarried, pregnant governess and neither could she return home to France as this would bring great shame to the family.

Something snapped inside Lucette, and the Petres' could sense the light had been blown out in this pretty young woman. She took to walking the Deer Park late at night, wandering to the spots where she would meet her lover and finally the bridge where they first kissed. She realised she was doomed and threw herself into the rushing torrents below.

She sealed her fate to eternally wander the house and grounds of Dunkenhalgh on the night of her death, Christmas Eve.

The Ghost Hunter in Dublin

Elliott O'Donnell was for many years Britain's leading ghost hunter, an author of over fifty books; he also wrote dozens of articles for newspapers and magazines. Sadly, he died in 1965, but his legacy continues with many ghost hunters influenced by his works.

In 1920 Elliot wrote about an alleged experience in Dublin when as he drove down Gloucester Street encountered a ghostly dog,

> We suddenly realised that we had witnessed the animal passing through a solid object. Both of us drove for a few seconds before saying anything, but we both realised something strange had happened. Hairs on the back of the neck and all that. We visited the building after the cinema and made sure that it was a door which indeed it was. The actual building was Hotspur house in Gloucester Street, the time we saw the dog was at 7:35pm on Thursday the 24th August.

On Christmas Eve, there was a wake "to celebrate Mr O'Donnell's ghost," Elliott continues his story,

> the dancing was at its height, when suddenly there came a loud knocking, and turning to the door, we saw the old hag again, who beckoned us. We followed her to an upstairs room, where a terrible sight met our gaze. Upon the floor lay the form of a singularly beautiful girl, and over her stood a man garbed in Cavalier dress, his sword dripping with blood. Then came a tremendous crash and everything disappeared. Only about half of us saw the apparition, but all heard the crash, for which no one was able to account. There was no more dancing that Christmas Eve!

Many claim that Elliott enhanced the truth of some of his stories; is the one you've just read the same? Or was Elliott a medium of some kind? He certainly admitted later in life that he thought he had the gift of second sight.

Found Lying By The Supper Table

Ghost stories can be pretty dark, and this is no exception. I warn you now that this is probably the darkest and most upsetting of all the stories in this book. If you want to keep that warm Christmas feeling, maybe skip this story until another time.

It was Christmas 1934, and journalist Bill Lockwood was sent to investigate a highly unusual death of a family.

I was involved in a real ghost story back in 1934,
it's all very well to say that the old, red-bricked
house is no more – The Germans blasted it out of
existence in the Blitz of 1944, so the haunted
house is no longer, and has since been replaced by
a block of luxury apartments.

I was asked to report on the mysterious death of a
family, they had been out for their Christmas Eve
celebration: mother, father, and their grown-up
son and two daughters. Their maid had left them
their supper and gone home, leaving a 'Merry
Christmas' message and saying she would be in
good time in the morning.

When the maid returned to the house on Christmas morning, she found the family sprawled over the supper table – all dead. Bill was sent to the house as he lived not too far away and was the closest journalist to get the 'scoop'.

"By the time we had got the details, Christmas Day
1934 was anything but a happy, restful one for us.
I discovered that the family had died in a suicide
pact.

Since I lived quite close by, I saw that year after
year, it stood empty, and I noticed that time took
down the curtains, decay made the shutters rattle
on windy nights as I passed, and the owls from

Streatham Common seemed to like the place. As the years passed, and the place got more neglected, the memory of that tragedy faded. Soon the 'To Let' board was replaced by one 'For Sale', and then one day that went too.

Neighbours heard that the Marchby family would be returning from South Africa to live in the home. Within a few hours of the family moving in, I was on the doorstep again; I thought there may be a story about South Africa.

Hugo Marchby, the head of the family, showed me into the room on the right, the very room where, years ago, I had described that first tragedy. I met his wife, and presently there were the girls Yolanda and Edis. Things were looking much the same as they did with previously, and when they told me that Denny, their son, had gone to London, I gave a silent 'Phew' but whispered not a word. It was just like that other family dead around the table in that very room so many years ago. Only now there was no table, and the room was now a lounge. All I hoped was that people would ever tell them what I knew and dare not tell them. But somebody did.

Yes, they got to know alright, and the ghost story begins here. For the Marchbys, the house was always haunted, as it had been for all those years, although I saw no ghost, they did. What happened next still shakes me today; something unnatural took place without a doubt. Within a few weeks, I saw the family change; the girls looked fearsome to return home, they looked troubled. Edis was the first to die, nobody knew what happened, but she babbled that she had seen something the night before. I went to the crematorium with her sister Yolanda. Aside from the grieving, she had concerns about the house. She blamed it for her sister's death. Not many months later, Yolanda went out of her mind; I never knew what became of her and then the mother died. For the boy, Denny, there was another end, and the bomb that fell on the house that fateful November night in 1944 killed him and his father. It's funny how things happen like that on our doorstep, and we think nothing of them until we piece the bits of the jigsaw together at Christmas when the wind blows eerily, the fire sparks up and dies down again. It's nearly time for bed.

A Sermon For The Spirits

Many books detail the ghost of Beaulieu and its famous National Motor Museum. Set in the New Forest National Park, the Beaulieu estate includes the village of Buckler's Hard, Palace House and Beaulieu Abbey. Originally a gatehouse to Beaulieu Abbey founded by King John in 1204, the house is haunted by 'Black Monks', rambling nuns and a myriad of characters throughout history.

In 1952 the National Motor Museum was opened by estate owner Lord Montagu and at its helm as curator was Charles Beatty. In a candid interview, Charles said that his marriage to novelist Joan Grant broke down due to the interactions of the 'ghost of Abbot Hugh', the resident ghost of the estate. Interestingly Joan became famous while living at Beaulieu for her book "The Winged Pharoah" – which for twenty years she kept secret that she had 'channelled' the material during meditation and séances!

Beaulieu's Christmas ghosts seem a communicative lot. Between 1886 and 1939, the last Vicar of Beaulieu, Reverend Robert Powles, claimed that the ghosts were an everyday part of his life. Often, he was known to make comments to parishioners such as, "Brother Simon was here again last night. I heard his boots squeak".

By the 1930s, the Vicar began to organise special midnight masses for the ghosts on Christmas Eve.

Lord Montagu's eldest sister Elizabeth Varley knew Rev. Powles and once said of him, "he always appeared perfectly sane" and "seemed to be on good terms with the ghosts, whom he saw and spoke to regularly". Looking back at the activities of the Reverend Powles, did he really witness ghosts daily and did anybody else see them with him?

And the final question, was the chapel full of ghosts on his midnight masses on Christmas Eve?

The Phantom Lorry

The New Inn and the A57 road between Sheffield and Manchester provide an excellent introduction to the hauntings of this incredibly active 'window' area known for its UFO, ghost and strange encounters.

In the early days, The New Inn was a farmhouse licensed in the mid-1800s to a Robert Turner. Many ramblers and travellers on the way to the Derbyshire hills and beyond would stop at the Inn. One such traveller became its landlord; Samuel Swann was a well-known personality in the area and reputedly the strongest man in Cheshire. Locals claimed he was a giant with a huge chest, and he could grasp a pint pot and crush it in his grip. By 1960 the area was transformed by the construction of the Hattersley estate, and the New Inn changed from a country inn to a local pub for hundreds of inhabitants. Sadly, in the 1960s, the Inn had the gruesome distinction of looking on to the house on Wardle Brook Avenue (now demolished), which was the scene of the infamous "Moors Murders".

In the 1920s, the A57 (or the Manchester to Sheffield Road) became known to have a 'haunted spot' on a stretch of road with The New Inn at its centre.

Sadly, over a two-year period from 1928 to 1930, there were dozens of accidents on this stretch, often with the same underlying theme – that the accident was caused by a phantom lorry reversing onto the road. Not only that, but most accidents happened near Christmas!

During the inquest into the death of Charles Ridgeway, who died due to injuries he received in an accident while riding in a motorcycle sidecar driven by his cousin Albert Collinson, several witnesses were asked to provide evidence. Collinson claimed that while travelling near the New Inn, he suddenly saw a large vehicle backing out of a side lane but remembered nothing more. And yet other witnesses declared they saw no other vehicle; the Coroner implied there was something curious about the road and the manner of the accidents happening.

The New Inn and its hauntings were also brought to the spotlight by locals discussing the 'strangeness' in the area. It was claimed that cars left standing outside the New Inn had been known to start suddenly off down the road ten minutes after the engines had been stopped.

The then landlord, William Gatton, also admitted the area was indeed haunted and that he and his neighbours had heard voices for the last six years. One of the neighbours, Mrs Simister, became so terrified of hearing heavy footsteps during the night that she had to leave her bungalow. She often woke screaming when she heard the footsteps and heard men talking amongst themselves.

Things came to a head in February 1930 during the Charles Ridgeway inquest when the Coroner asked members of the jury to investigate the spot where the phantom lorry had appeared. They were quickly joined by packs of journalists and then a crowd of spiritualists. One newspaper wrote,

> Mr. W.Baten, the well-known spiritualist, tried again to induce some psychic manifestation. Near the spot where a series of fatal accidents have occurred, Mr Baten broke a hawthorn twig and remained silent. The twig did not move, but the party shivered – with the cold.

It is a shame that in the 1930s, the journalists did not vigil in the New Inn itself – the pub boasts a ghost in the shape of an old woman known as Mary. She was reputedly a cleaner at the inn in the last century and is sometimes heard scrubbing the floors in the toilets and, according to one landlord, walks the corridors, swishing her skirt.

Sadly, in August 2012, the New Inn was demolished to make way for a new housing development – will the phantom lorry and Mary make themselves known to the new tenants?

The Ghost Hunting Miners

A highly active poltergeist became the undoing of four miners when they investigated a haunted farmhouse in Brierley, West Yorkshire.

It was Christmas 1902, and Farmer Laybourne's house had become well known in the area for being haunted. The spectre was said to reside in the washhouse, and for a long time, the 'dolly tubs' and other washing appliances were witnessed jumping around and being thrown to the floor. Clothes leapt about the washhouse and even seen flying up the chimney!

On one occasion, the washtub was found overturned, and after it had been put back, a little while later, the mysterious force once again overturned the tub.

In the main house, items of furniture and ornaments had been seen dancing around while the cushions were thrust into the fireplace several times. It was only a matter of time that the family moved out, and sure enough, a few days after Christmas, they left.

However, Farmer Laybourne and his farm servant stood their ground. Soon the fame of the ghost spread throughout the district, with large crowds visiting the haunted house with the hope of either 'laying the ghost' or even witnessing its incredible feats.

After a few days, the crowds had reached such a size that Laybourne applied for police protection, sadly the police did not catch the ghost, but four miners were caught eating Mr Laybourne's supper.

The four men had been found 'ghost seeking' while drinking copious amounts of alcohol and being comfortably ensconced in the kitchen eating Laybourne's supper!

The men were brought before the West Riding bench at Barnsley charged with being found on the premises of Mr Laybourne and eating a couple of chops and a cutlet. Although the miners claimed they had no intention of damaging the house, they claimed they were frightened to stay at Laybourne's house.

"I do not believe in ghosts," said one of the defendants, "and I went to stay until midnight, but instead of the ghost, it was the constable who came."

Each of the men was fined forty shillings and costs, and no further mention of Laybourne's poltergeist can be found.

The Missouri Wild Man

Strangeness can linger in a town like the early morning frost of Autumn. In 1883, a quiet and religious township was enveloped in mystery and terror. Mexico, Missouri, gained its name to capitalise on the popularity of Texas joining the union, and in the 1880s, it was a small thriving settlement of around 6000 inhabitants.

On the eve of Thanksgiving 1883, a portent of the coming strangeness appeared to two gentle folks in the neighbourhood around Hopewell Church, a few miles west of Mexico.

Mr Cyrus Haggert and his wife, who was travelling on thanksgiving eve, were the first to encounter the supernatural being. Returning from the church that night, they were surprised by the monster's peering with its cat-like eyes into their buggy and leaning against it, almost crushing the vehicle. The couple took many weeks to recover from their experience, claiming that they had seen an eight-foot to ten-foot, lean, monster man wearing a long cloak, with his head bowed in an abstracted way. The monster was claimed to have had small, glittering eyes resembling a cat or some wild beast. Little did the residents around Hopewell Church realise that the monster's appearances would increase over the following months.

Just before Christmas, John Creasy, a well-respected resident, who fought as a soldier under General Grant in the Civil War, encountered the beast. Returning from Mexico in the late afternoon, he had a good view of the strange being who was about fifty yards ahead of him, walking in a leisurely way along the middle of the road, almost knee-deep in mud. John described the entity as wearing a long flowing black cloak and walking with his head lowered. All at once, the monster disappeared in the thick woods as mysteriously as he came upon the scene. Creasy told local newspapers that even though he had fought in Civil War for the first time in his life, he was really frightened, and it took all he could do to control his horse, so great was its fear of the object.

Further sightings of this incredible were recorded, but the folk of Hopewell Church could not decide if they had experienced a strange creature or a ghost. With this in mind, a large party gathered led by Bob White, a local politician and Jake Merkell, a farmer, as well as being joined by several journalists, took to hunting down the creature. A local tracker claimed that the monster lived in the hills behind the farm of a Mr Philip Brown, and so the hunt set out to find this terrifying creature.

It was supposed that the habitation of the monster was pretty definitely known, and little doubt existed that the wild man, or whatever the thing may be, had a home in a cave in the hills but recently discovered, but this was proved a mistake. The cave was searched thoroughly, but no evidence found that it has been made a home by anything but wild animals, which are plentiful in the woods of the region.

A few days later, Anton Bradshaw was returning from town late when he saw it sitting bolt upright on the fence in front of Hopewell Church, with its head bowed, apparently meditating. With quick thinking,

Anton turned his horse's head and ran back to shelter at a neighbour's home. After this sighting, Hopewell Church and its school were abandoned because of the fear of the monster, and even armed farmers refused to venture outside at night.

Over Christmas 1883, there are several reports of sightings, including the aforementioned Bob White mistaking a shadow for a ghost at Hopewell Church and fainting in front of a large crowd.

In January 1884, the son of John Creasy, contacted the Mexico Weekly Ledger that he had discovered a large coat. While hunting deer near Hopewell Church, he believed he had found the coat of the 'wild man', it was alleged to have been made up of many skins – bear, buffalo, elephant, kangaroo, and tiger – whether this was an embellishment of John Junior or the newspaper, is unclear.

It seems that the Wildman sightings stopped for a few months, and there certainly are no reports in any local newspapers, just vignettes that 'something' local was happening. Local hunting parties organised by wealthy benefactors and organisations continued to look for the wild man, but no apparent result.

Then, on August 28th, 1884, the Mexico Weekly Ledger published a small news item,

> We understand that John Creasy has bought the 'haunted hill' immediately west of Philip Brown's residence.

One of the greatest annoyances of being a paranormal researcher of old newspapers and documents is the lack of ability to see what was really happening. What was the 'Haunted Hill', was it linked to the cave behind Philip Brown's farm, and how did it relate to the wild man? The next stage of activity was just about to start, the newspaper article read,

Numerous Wrecks on a Road near Where a Ghost was Rudely Investigated

Out in what is known as the 'ghost district' west of Mexico, Missouri, it would seem a fated hill, over which traverses the main county road. In a conversation this morning with a well-known farmer who resides in the vicinity (Philip Brown?), he stated that within the past year, there had been no less than fifty disastrous runways on this particular hill and that old fragments of wagons and buggies could be seen lying around in all directions. Several persons, too, have been injured, the result of teams of horses becoming frightened and tearing at breakneck speed down the narrow, perpendicular space.

Who or what was causing these crashes, and why did they start after the wild man sightings? As with many cases of the paranormal, sometimes the activity can change format or develop over time.

The haunted hill continued to claim many victims. Two young ladies, the Misses Stevens, were thrown out of their buggy on Haunted Hill, one of them sustaining a severe ankle fracture. In this instance, the buggy was smashed. One earlier witness to the wild man, Anton Bradshaw and his family were returned home when their two workhorses took fright and ran away, luckily injuring no one but literally demolishing the vehicle.

Poor Issac Reed was another who experienced the terror of Haunted Hill. He passed close to the hill and let his horse drink from the ford on the way home. Suddenly his horse gave a fearful lunge, bucking and tearing around a fearful rate, and it was some time before the animal could be calmed. What the horse saw or heard, Mr Reed did not discover, and not long after this episode, his horse lay for an hour in a 'death-like' stupor only to recover.

Haunted Hill took on almost poltergeist level activity; Mr Childress, a respectable farmer, had his wagon upset by a 'mysterious power' that dumped his provisions into the creek at the foot of the hill and was swept away. Mr Childress was able to rescue his horses, who, like Issac Reed's, went mad.

The wild man also returned to the vicinity of Hopewell Church just a few days before Christmas, 1884.

> A well-known gentleman of this city (Mexico, Missouri), driving over the road at nightfall encountered an apparition gigantic in height, ethereal in substance, long cloaked and booted, which approached and rest familiarly on the box of his buggy. It kept pace with a rapid, and in this case an exceedingly terrified horse, and then disappeared, how or whence the gentleman was perhaps in no condition to discover.

Local newspapers reported that the Haunted Hill should not be travelled at night; it should 'not even be contemplated' wrote journalists. Some newspapers blamed the ghost for the accidents on the hill and even created incredible descriptions of his alleged appearance, "He is mounted on a 'pale horse', he is a gigantic figure, clad in pure white, apparently floating in the air, he is a grisly skeleton, surmounted by a ghastly death's-head in the shape of an especially horrible, grinning skull."

Another local newspaper wrote,

> the haunted hill is situated two miles west of Mexico, Missouri in the 'ghost district' which derived its name last fall from a strange creature roaming at large, it is said, through the wood of the locality, frightening the inhabitants nearly out of their wits, and which mystery never was fathomed, although day after day and night after night hunting parties were out scouring the thickly wooded, sparsely settled neighbourhood. The haunted hill, as they call it, is merely a sequence to the appearance of the mysterious personage of last fall.

In my personal research of ghost cases, I find that a singular event can cause a series of both paranormal and unusual human activity within a small area. As we can see with the neighbourhood of Hopewell

Church, the wild man sightings were a catalyst to continued unusual activity, sparking the haunted hill where numerous horse-related accidents took place but also strange 'human' encounters such as this story,

> Last Sunday evening Jimmy Jesse, who lives right
> in the heart of the ghost district, was returning
> home and when near the haunted hill, he was met
> by three unknown men who made him dismount
> from his horse. All three men then got on the
> animal and went up the haunted hill at break-neck
> speed. After a diligent search, they found the horse
> to the rear of Philip Brown's residence.

Once again, the mystery slips into the dark. The reports of unusual activity disappear from the newspapers; however, there are further insights into the Haunted Hill and the hauntings three years later. The Mexico Weekly Ledger once again covered the story in December 1888.

Is Haunted Hill Deserted?

> History of the Famous Hill and Its Mystery For
> years, the Hill was known to be haunted. With the
> coming of the first frost in September, great
> moanings and wailings would emanate from the
> mysterious Hill, and belated travellers would at
> night hear terrible noises and witness blood-
> curdling sightings in the strip of woods that cover
> the wonderful place. Strong men of courage
> frequently equipped themselves with weapons and
> armour and would endeavour to drive from their
> haunts the mysterious being that made Haunted
> Hill their nightly rendezvous. But it was always in
> vain; the parties always returned empty-handed.

The journalist continues that rather than a series of small encounters, that "year after year the ghosts held high carnival, with the coming of frost, and until late the next year, the Hill was a place of terror."

The article then mentions John Creasy, who is mentioned several times in the articles over the five years of reporting the wild man and haunted hill. After researching the area around Hopewell Church, John seems to have owned the land directly at the back of the church and no doubt would have been highly affected by the wild man's actions.

> It was about three years ago, and John, who then lived in the Ghost District, who took a band of ghost hunters up Haunted Hill but returned back in the morning unrewarded. All the fall and winter passed, and there were no supernatural manifestations. The delightful mystery surrounding the Haunted Hill and Ghost Hollow still existed but grew no deeper. Another winter came, and no more ghosts.
>
> Only the legend remained.

And like many true-life stories, that is the end of this particular story.

A few things I noted is that many of the witnesses of the wild man were armed farmers. If this was some sort of persistent hoax, then whoever was the perpetrator or perpetrators would have been risking being injured or killed. Several times armed gangs went hunting for the wild man. If a hoaxer was behind it, I can only imagine what these gangs would have done if they had discovered them. That is one of the reasons why I believe this is a very genuine and unusual case, especially when the activity begins at the 'Haunted Hill'. Like the wild man sightings, witnesses to the haunted hill experiences included politicians, well-respected gentlemen and armed farmers. Usually, in cases from the 1800s, there is a strong sceptical streak that will insinuate that the ghost case is fake – while some blame is thrown in the direction of John Creasy, I doubt this to be the case.

Reviewing where the sightings and haunted hill experiences took place, we are not talking about a built-up area, just a few farms scattered over five miles square. Furthermore, we can see that some of the witnesses and their families owned the land in the area. Suppose the son or a family relative was discovered to be behind this reoccurring, five-year mystery? In that case, this close-knit, church-going community would have been literally shattered – again, who would have risked this with a simple prank?

Out of the high weirdness cases of this book, all the US-based ghost stories are very unusual, but not if we compare with high strangeness cases of Bigfoot, UFO and hauntings. From 1973 through 1974 in Pennsylvania, ufologist Stan Gordon was swamped with countless UFO sightings with high strangeness. Remote farms claimed to have seen UFOs and Bigfoot, a multitude of descriptions and experiences. Some claimed Men in Black visitations, poltergeist activity and even strange animal deaths. And like the Missouri wild man and the Haunted Hill, the cases suddenly stopped without explanation.

So was the wild man a ghost, a bigfoot or something else? Did he trigger the Haunted Hill sightings? For sure, we will never know, and as the Mexico Weekly Ledger wrote, "no more ghosts. Only the legend remained."

Murder In Stoke Poges

For over a hundred and fifty years, an old woman's ghost haunts the village of Stoke Poges in South Buckinghamshire. In the middle of the village is a large, old house, now used as the infant school, that was once a shop. The house had the reputation of being haunted for many years by the restless spirit of Nanny Smith, who, based on the local tradition, was murdered there.

She was the proprietor of what we would now call a general store – a place where you could buy anything you wanted at any time you wanted. The shop was very successful, and it also became well known in the neighbourhood that Nanny Smith had received a great deal of money through an inheritance.

On Christmas Morning in 1849, Nanny's servant girl came to take down the shutters and open the shop. However, when she opened the door, she discovered her mistress' dead body lying across the floor in a pool of blood. Her skull fractured as if hit by something incredibly heavy and blunt.

Suspicion fell on a shoemaker who lived on the same street, and after intense pressure from his wife, he admitted his guilt. He had broken into her house to find the inheritance money, but she discovered him searching through her documents. In the heat of the burglary, he hit poor Nanny's head with his shoemaker's hammer smashing her skull and sending her to the floor.

The mystery of the lost money was never cleared up, and the house became the scene of a nocturnal haunting on Christmas Eve. Strange stories still linger about the old woman's ghost seen standing in the windows or walking across the street. In the late 1800s, her ghost had 'moved' to haunt a bend in nearby Plough Lane after a series of sightings by several villagers. Strangely, in 1898 two old women mistook an old donkey walking around in a neighbouring field as the ghost of Nanny Smith, thinking that the donkey's twitching tail was Nanny's arm!

The Ghostly Dr Astley

A spectral visitor came to the home of Reverend Brock on 26th December 1908. The tale is guaranteed to send a shiver down your spine.

Reverend Brock was the Acting Vicar of East Rudham near King's Lynn, Norfolk. East Rudham is a quaint and ancient village not known for paranormal activity. However, an incredible story took place a few days before Christmas at the Old Rectory in the village.

The time approached four in the afternoon, and the winter's sun was slowly setting across the rectory's lawn. Suddenly the housekeeper shouted to Reverend Brock, "Come and see Dr Astley!" Brock did not believe his housekeeper as Dr Astley was the Vicar of the parish but had left to go overseas. The Reverend met his housekeeper in the study and looked out of the window across the lawn but saw nothing.

"You are looking in the wrong direction!" exclaimed the housekeeper.

Brock turned to his right and saw a clergyman with a white-collar gleaming in the gathering darkness. He instantly thought it must be a reflection of himself. However, this was impossible from the position he was situated.

The vision presented itself as a clergyman sitting at a table or desk with books before him. The 'ghost' wore a gold chain across his waistcoat, exactly how Dr Astley wore his. Brock took four or five views before rushing outside to the supposed wall against which the figure was sitting. When he reached the wall, he discovered that the ghost had been sitting in a small outlet or alcove; the housekeeper remarked that it was where Dr Astley would sit in summer to read.

Dr Astley, the Vicar of East Rudham, left the village on 10th December. Unbeknownst to Brock and the Housekeeper, Dr Astley and his wife had been killed in a railway accident in Algiers. This was only confirmed weeks after the sighting of the Vicar on the lawn.

The Riderless Horses of Copyhold Lane

Butler's Green, a small village that sits on the old coaching road between Cuckfield and Haywards Heath, Sussex, seems to be the epicentre of paranormal activity that has lasted for hundreds of years. Sporadic hauntings across the Mid Sussex landscape are seemingly linked by the route of a stampede of phantom horses that appear on moonlit nights between Christmas and the New Year.

> They do not appear every year, but at irregular and sometimes long intervals, but always on a moonlight night. They are said to favour a misty moon when there is a tang in the night wind and just enough to curdle the air into a beautiful white rime.

HUBERT BATES, WATCHMAKER, BUTLERS GREEN 1938

I cannot imagine anything more terrifying than hearing the thundering sound of horses' hooves on a small, unlit country lane in the middle of the night. The fear that you would be about to be trampled by a real stampede, and the real-life danger it brings, to discovering that it was a ghost herd (or team) of horses.

Pre-1900s, wandering down ancient Copyhold Lane on a moonlight night would not be helped by streetlights, and the calming light of the moon would not provide help on a muddy track surrounded by tall hedges. The fear that you could encounter the Riderless Horses would have kept most villagers safely in their homes over the Christmas holidays.

Digging through the country of Sussex's long history and folklore, from the early 18th Century, the ghostly horses are said to have made their ghastly route across the countryside on or around New Year's Eve. At the same time, some sources claim only on a moonlight night during this time. What is known is where the horses start their run just a few miles from Butlers Green in the village of Anstye, an ancient village with hints of a prehistoric lineage.

A local hill, 'Mount Noddy', is believed to have been named after the Celtic Deity, Nodens, coincidentally or not, the God of hunting and dogs.

"The ghostly horses run across the meadow from
the nearby village of Anstye and down the old
bridle path...."

Hubert Bates, watchmaker and teacher, was known locally for knowing
Cuckfield's history and folklore. He wrote many letters to the Mid-
Sussex Times, and in these letters, he inadvertently preserved traditions
and stories from Mid-Sussex.

He wrote extensively about the Riderless Horses, and he believed the
horses began their gallop just outside Anstye Farm. A fine old period
Sussex farmhouse, its interior is rich in oak and possibly dates to the
Tudors. The old farmhouse is said to be haunted by an exhausted-
looking male figure who walks the bridlepath, probing the hedge with
a rake in search of, local folklore says, of lost deed hidden centuries
ago in a hole by the roadside. If you ever encounter this frustrated
ghost who continues his search long after his death, he is dressed in
dark clothing with a leather satchel slung across his shoulders. And yet,
just a few feet away, the stampede begins.

To travel from Ansty to Butlers Green using a car and the new bypass
would take 4 minutes, but cross country, on a horse at full pelt, it must
have taken around 10 to 15 minutes to travel the 2.2 miles between the
locations.

"down the old bridle path the horses go,
thundering through Furnace Wood, they turn
sharply on to Copyhold Lane."

A 'Copyhold' is a very old term meaning that the land was owned by
the Manor, and that manor, in this case, was Butlers Green House –
the destination of the horses at the end of this Romanesque straight
country lane.

The route of the Horses is unusually physical and grounded. Across
Europe, there are countless tales and folkloric stories of the 'Wild
Hunt', but usually, they are aerial, and not as grounded as these
thundering mares. The Wild Hunt historically occurs in the folklore
of Northern Europe and usually includes a chase led by a mythological

figure escorted by a ghostly group of hunters, horses, and dogs. Gwyn Ap Nudd, who bears similarities to the aforementioned Nodens, has several Welsh and Gloucestershire stories of running Wild Hunts across the skies of Glastonbury and other locations. Is there some link to these stories and Butlers Green?

> "onto Copyhold Lane onto Cuckfield Road. Then they turn and gallop madly up the road to Butler's Green."

And so, they reach their destination, Butlers Green House. The initial house was built around the 14th century and then repeatedly modified and expanded from this point. The 'House' looks like several buildings from Elizabethan all the way through to Georgia, and around the 1600s, the main house was built for the old Sussex family, The Botelers. Over time Boteler's Green became Butler's Green. There is scant information about its inhabitants before the Boteler family, but its most famous ghost (aside from the phantom horses) is the Grey Lady.

The Grey Lady of Butlers Green House seems to have links with the Riderless Horses, so I'll share the story. There are numerous references to this tragic ghost, many dating back to the 19th and 18th Centuries.

The story is often repeated or even applied by storytellers around Britain to a 'grey lady ghost'.

Many years ago, when she was alive, the grey lady was married to a man of wild talents. He was a gambler, violent and passionate, but above all, he was extremely jealous. During one of these temper tantrums, he stabbed his wife, who was trying to protect their child. She ran out of the house in her blood-stained grey dress, carrying her baby in sheer terror, looking for help. She passed through the big old estate gates, and then, it is believed that she drowned herself and her baby in the pond next to the old lime tree terrace. No one knows for sure whether she was drowned at the hands of the violent husband or a tragic accident as the blood drained away from her, causing her to fall.

However, within a few years, it became apparent that the old estate gates were haunted, and that the Grey Lady had placed a curse on them. If anyone should ever pass through the gates, a death would occur in the household within the year, so concerned locals locked and chained them, and the owners of Butlers Green House arranged for another entrance.

The Grey Lady is often reported to haunt the grounds occasionally. In 1942 a young musician saw the ghost and told her story to the Mid Sussex Times.

> It was a brilliantly moonlit night, and I approached Butlers Green about 8 o'clock. As I reached Butlers Green House, a figure which I took to be a nun – she wore a mediaeval grey costume, passed right in front of my front wheel as made for the direction of the pond. I tried to dodge her, and she was not there! Getting off my cycle, I walked to the edge of the pond and stared down at it. I could see nothing.

> Later, when I reached Cuckfield, I told my experience to two friends, they told me that I had seen the Butler's Green Ghost. It was the first time I had heard about the ghost, so the story could not have influenced me and made me fancy I saw the figure. I was so frightened when told about the ghost I could not travel down the road again unless accompanied. Curiously enough, the late Mr Simmins had a similar experience about the same time on a summer's night. While walking to Cuckfield, he saw what he thought was a nun in

grey proceeding from the house towards the pond,
and on the way back, he saw her returning. She
appeared to pass right through the fence.

The newspaper claimed the ghost had not been seen for many a year, and no living person has ever seen the old gates to Butlers Green House unlocked. Like the Lane Ghost of Anstye, is there a connection to the phantom horses or each other?

On the last stroke of midnight on a moonlight
night between Christmas and the New Year, a
ghostly troop of grey, riderless horses appear..they
enter (literally) through the old estate gates (Grey
Lady's cursed gates) and rush to the old stables,
and there they scrape the brick paving, paw on the
gravel and whinny in the most unearthly manner.

If at this moment, a person opens the stable doors, the phantom horses pass in, and no more is seen or heard of them, but if they fail to awake and not open the doors, then the horses turn around frantically, run through the old gates, down the Cuckfield Road, and disappear into Copyhold Lane, and so return to Anstye.

But this comes with a dire warning; the failure to allow the horses in means that "before another New Year's Eve is past, a blight falls on some unfortunate individual sleeping that night at Butlers Green."

Hubert concluded in one letter, "No one knows what frightful tragedy lies behind this weird visitation, but the seriousness of the crime is evident by all the horses being riderless."

A real ghost story never has a conclusion; that is the nature of the paranormal. There is no doubt that the Riderless Horses was known and experienced for hundreds of years in the area. The stories passed on from generation to generation, but could the stories of this ride be much older – linked to the Wild Hunt?

To encounter the Wild Hunt was a presage to an unfortunate event such as war, disease, or even your own death, but also there are stories that you could be abducted by the Wild Hunt. While the Riderless Horses and the people of Butlers Green rely on someone opening the stables doors to remain safe, there is that fear that the horses will return to Anstye and a death will occur in the village.

To me, there seems to be a link at least in its origin but what intrigues me more is that at the beginning and the end of the route are ghost stories. Britain and many other countries have invisible lines linking paranormal and unusual activity. Some call them 'ley lines', but this seems all too easy. My feelings are that an area can become clustered with unusual activity over time.

Here with Butlers Green, we have two different aged ghost stories linked by possibly an older, mythological ghost story. Whatever your thoughts are for this story, we cannot dismiss that statistically on paper, these three stories shouldn't be linked, so is there is a darker origin story that we are simply unaware of?

The Ghost Of The Warrior

A weird Christmas tale comes from the little County Tyrone town of Newtownstewart in Northern Ireland. The town is overlooked by hills named "Bessy Bell and Mary Gray" after two Perthshire gentlemen' daughters.

> And Bessy Bell and Mary Gray, They war twa
> bonnie lasses; They biggit a bower on yon burn-
> brae, And theekit it oer wi rashes.

A local ballad says that in 1666, girls built themselves a small bower to avoid catching the plague that ravished across the country. The girls were supplied by a local boy who had fallen in love with them, and sadly the lad caught the plague and gave it to the girls. All three sickened and died, so the hills were named after the 'twa bonnie lassies".

When Scottish migrants reached Staunton, Virginia, two hills were named after the girls; others exist in New Zealand. The Newtownstewart hills are said to be very weird and an uneasy place to visit, with some claiming to have seen the shadowy, wispy white figures of the two girls wandering the hills.

If Newtownstewart wasn't strange enough, in the 1800s, the town inhabitants were well known for believing in supernatural visitations. One Christmas, the town had a special visitor, possibly one of Royal Lineage!

Situated near the Old Corn Market is Newtownstewart Castle on Townhall Street. Only the South and North Walls still stan, but the castle's archways were used as the town marketplace in the 19th century.

Interestingly, Newtownstewart Castle has also the distinction of being the site of a significant Bronze Age discovery: An intact double cist grave and capstone.

In 1906, the locals were shocked by the appearance of a glowing ghost wearing a suit of chainmail. On the Saturday night before Christmas, townsfolk encountered a strange apparition standing at the Corn Market gate – one of the castle's old arches. The party of people were naturally perturbed by the encounter, and one of the witnesses addressed the ghostly knight and asked what he wanted? The spectre deigned not to reply and promptly disappeared.

Soon the story of the strange happenings spread like wildfire across town, many scoffed at the sightings, but a day later, the sceptics soon changed their minds.

At Midnight on Sunday, a great ringing of bells was distinctly heard across the district, and several persons looking out to discover the cause of the unwanted sounds saw, to their amazement, the mail-clad figure standing at the entrance of the castle – but this time with a bright light shining all around it.

Once again, curious inhabitants set out to interview the 'ghostly knight', and before they could reach the spot, he had disappeared. His final appearance came a day later when the knight was seen again visiting the arches of the castle. And with that, the ghost of 1906 disappeared, literally and was never reported again.

Was it a hoax or maybe, a genuine 'ghost' visiting on an important anniversary? Nobody knows for sure. However, 92 years later, two archaeologists discovered two cremated skeletons, one adult, the other believed to be a teenager, on the spot where the ghost appeared. Rather than being a 'knight', was the ghost an Iron Age warrior?

The Green Lady

Mary Queen of Scots seems to haunt several locations across England and Scotland, one of which is situated on the Fife coast, the picturesque Wemyss Castle.

The construction of the present castle dates to 1421, when Sir John Wemyss replaced an earlier one destroyed by the Duke of Rothesay in 1402. The castle is the ancient seat of the Earls of Wemyss and the Clan Wemyss. Historically the castle is best known as the meeting place of Mary Queen of Scots and her future husband, Lord Darnley, in 1565.

The Green Lady has been seen numerous times over the last two hundred years, and there has always been the conjecture that she is Mary, Queen of Scots. During the 1800s, a famed Scots minister was leaving the castle after a party on Christmas Eve. As he reached the end of the drive, he paused and looked back to get a view of the castle in the snow by night. As he observed the site, he saw the Green Lady flittering around the walls. He told his companion to look, and they both saw the Lady disappear, walking slowly round to the side of the castle which faces the sea.

As with many mansions and castles across Britain, the castle was sequestered as a hospital during the First World War. During this time, many people lay claim to witnessing the Green Lady; one nurse had a very good sighting. While returning to the castle to complete her shift, the nurse was passed by a lady in a green cloak in one of the passages. Wondering who the unauthorised visitor could be, she followed the lady and attempted to catch up with her. When she reached the corner of the passage, the visitor had disappeared.

Death By Fright

This sad Christmas ghost story comes from Greenhill Lane, near Alfreton, Derbyshire. A night of ghost stories turned to one of manslaughter in a story that sent a shock and controversy around the country.

Just a few days before Christmas 1856, Robert Mitchell, a fifteen-year-old agricultural worker, visited the farmhouse of Mr Day to chat with his friends Issac Hudson and Jack Percival. He spent a couple of hours with the two boys and their masters Mr and Mrs Day, telling tales about some (ghostly) knocks that they had been frightened with. During the chat, Percival and Hudson arranged, unknown to Mitchell, that they would play a trick and scare Mitchell once he left.

It was agreed that Percival would play the ghost and took a white tablecloth to put over himself and planned not to stand too far from the house when Mitchell left. About half-past seven, Percival told Hudson he was ready to leave, so Percival hid in the yard waiting for Hudson to bring out Mitchell fifteen minutes later, carrying the white tablecloth under his arm. Hudson did as planned and took Mitchell outside, saying that he would walk with Mitchell to the next farmhouse as the lane was haunted. As they got 120 yards from the house, Hudson saw Percival dressed in the white tablecloth. Jokingly Hudson shouted, "Look, Robert, what's that?" Robert replied, "Nothing comes along."

As Hudson and Mitchell approached Percival, Hudson feigned a scream and the 'ghost' walked across the lane and to a stile. Mitchell shouted, "Jack!" There was no answer. Mitchell shouted again, "Jack!" Again, no reply but this time, Percival made a groan. Mitchell shouted out, "Is it, Jack?" And again, Percival gave out a ghostly moan.

Percival then ran off, and Robert walked home, where he was in a terrified state. During the inquest, it was reported, "He was all of a tremble, looked white, and stared wildly and on being interrogated by his father related what had occurred, though he did not believe it to be Percival and he could not remember how he got home."

Robert Mitchell then deteriorated and refused to eat and went to bed. The next day he began vomiting and complained of a pain in his throat. Through the following day, he became worse and raved in his bed about what had happened, sadly dying the evening after.

During an inquest into the death, Mr Belcher, a surgeon, believed that Mitchell had died of extreme nervous excitement, and his death resulted from exhaustion from the shock to the nervous system caused by the 'ghost sighting'.

The Coroner asked his jury for a verdict, and they said that because Percival had caused his friend's death, the verdict was manslaughter.

Less than a year later, a court agreed not to sentence Percival for his part in Mitchell's death, where usually Percival would have been expecting to be transported overseas or imprisoned with hard labour.

Terror in Carondelet

There are many tales of the Mistletoe Bride ghost story in the United Kingdom, and since the story is so widespread and known, I have purposely left it out of this collection of ghost stories.

In the 1800s, there was another well-known Christmas bride ghost story, and I'll share its grisly details here.

Carondelet is a very old neighbourhood in the extreme southeastern portion of St. Louis, Missouri. Carondelet is famous for its rich, cultural history that dates back to 1767 when the French man Clement Delor de Treget built the first house in the area.

Originally called 'Delor's Village', over time it became 'Catalan's Prairie', then 'Louisbourg' – probably after Louis XVI, the king of France. Later, Treget, wanting to renew his military commission, tried to flatter the Governor-General of Louisiana, Baron De Carondelet, and named his village after him. Treget received his commission in return.

In 1832, Carondelet was incorporated and then later annexed to St. Louis in 1870. A local journalist described the area;

> A strong undercurrent of superstition…pervades
> the public mind; Carondelet is a peculiarly prolific
> field for ghosts. The superstition was imbued into
> the popular mind by the remnants of the old
> original Spanish and French settlers, who
> generated their traditions and elaborated them, and
> then passed them down by the unwritten method
> until every old ruin, of which there are many, and
> every nook or corner has its specific legend.

St Louis Globe-Democrat in 1888

The journalist clearly understands the cultural melting pot; however, he dismisses the case as pure folklore.

The ghost's first appearance was July 1888; the baseball team 'Carondelet Unions' were practising in Carondelet Park when the Captain, Dennis O'Keefe, spied an unusual spectator perched in a tree nearby. He noticed that it was female and was wearing a white, flowing nightdress just before dusk.

> The case struck me as being remarkable. I finally
> asked Fred Duckett, the shortstop, who she was,
> and then Billy Westerman, the right fielder. Both
> looked at her and said they didn't know who it
> could be, at the same time directing at the
> attending of the rest and the bystanders to her.

The spectre was described by several witnesses as having a pretty face with long sweeping locks of chestnut brown hair. Witnesses thought it was unusual that a young woman should be outside so late with an escort.

The pitcher thought she was waving her hands in front of her face, so he promptly sent her a high right curve, but instead of catching it, it seemed to pass right through her head. The boys looked at each other and ran to investigate.

Within a few feet of the tree, she disappeared in a flash, and nothing could be seen of her.

The case takes a strange turn – even for a ghost story. Dennis told newspapers,

> Three of us had gathered beneath the railroad
> bridge at Loughborough Avenue, when suddenly
> she rushed right between us with a series of
> horrible shrieks, and left a wave of chill, cold air
> which made us shudder, disappearing apparently in
> the abutments of solid masonry which the
> structure rests.

At this point, I understand if you doubt Dennis's second part of the story, but it was verified by Deputy Sheriff Tucker. The ghost had been seen three times in total, with a penchant of appearing around 8:30 in the evening. Tucker was so convinced that he told reporters he

would take an oath in Court that it was a ghost, and secondly, it followed the same route every appearance.
And then the story goes cold..until Christmas time.

> The people of Carondelet are in a state of terror over the appearance of a genuine ghost. The ghost is a figure, a well-developed female, with a flowing, snowy white gown, sleeveless. Two luminous eyes appear in startling relief, but yet between them, however, is a great crevice cloved in the skull is discernible, which seems to divide and spread out the upper half of the head into two lobes and from which a current of bright red blood appears to flow, dyeing the white garment in irregular crimson streaks..

One witness Frank Strother told reporters he knew something strange was happening in the area when dogs made a strange noise every Sunday morning. At about 1 o'clock in the morning, dogs would suddenly rapidly run around his house, backwards and forwards, barking and snapping as if an intruder were nearby. For over an hour, the dogs would prolong their actions, gradually disappearing one at a time, sneaking away.

Frank's neighbours noted that there were always fewer dogs joining the rabble over the last few appearances. Strangely local Sheriffs were asked to investigate the great number of dogs that had died in the neighbourhood. Each corpse found was said to bore the impress of a slight feminine hand. Strangely the hair had fallen away, and the skin burnt to a crisp.

Once the neighbour's dog disappeared, only Strother's own dog stood between the house and the spectre. Sadly, and chillingly, Strother and his neighbours were powerless as they heard the dog combating the unearthly visitor savagely, and the ghost slapping it repeatedly, and with such force, the whacks could be heard echoing between the houses.

Carondelet was so terrified; a glimpse of the figure was seen as a warning sign, and people would run to their homes for security. One woman witnessed the ghost when it peered over her shoulder while hanging out clothes on the washing line. Even though it was daylight, the witness clearly saw the horrid apparition, bedabbled in blood, watching.

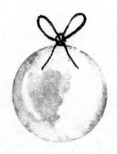

The Haunting Returned

I have often wondered why a haunting stops or dissolves into time. Famous ghost stories such as 50 Berkeley Square or Godolphin House have an alleged history of hauntings, yet nothing over the last seventy years. Do ghosts run out of energy, or is there something else at work?

Circleville in Ohio, probably best known for its Circleville Pumpkin Show – which sounds great – is built on native American land. In fact, its name refers to the original layout of the town, which was laid out in the circle of a Hopewell tradition earthwork. In the centre of the innermost circle was built the County Courthouse, the location of our next chilling story.

The Christmas ghost of Circleville is lost in time, and thorough research of Circleville's hauntings suggest that the ghost is no longer active – or maybe no longer reported? Either way, the ghost story seemingly has an ancient origin. Looking at the map of G.W.Wittich (below) we can clearly see the County Courthouse in the centre of the

Wittich, G. W. Circleville Illustrated. [Circleville, Ohio: s.n., 1878] Map. Retrieved from the Library of Congress, www.loc.gov/item/2011592044/

circle where once stood a large, central prehistoric mound surrounded by a series of earthworks.

The mound was around 15 feet in height and 60 feet in diameter. When excavated before the construction of the Courthouse, the mound was found to contain several burials and artefacts. On the top of this mound, there was an altar as historians believed it to be, and many locals believed that its destruction caused the ghost.

In 1840 there were several reports of hauntings since the Courthouse's construction, which was only thirty years old. However, a tradition had set in, and the townsfolk believed that a ghost would appear every Christmas. The appearance of the ghost was very real to the early settlers who built their homes on and around those ancient walls and earthworks.

One reporter told of the tradition of a ghost standing on Court and Main Street, but only on Midnight Christmas Eve and this belief lasted until the end of the century.

But the enchanting stories of this Christmas ghost disappeared with the original courthouse when it was rebuilt in 1846, and there are no records of his appearance since then.

While the trail of this Christmas ghost disappears (or does it), Cameron Jones, a resident of Mound Street, just a block away from the Courthouse, believes that activity in his home increases at Christmas.

Yet when I contacted him, he was unaware of the obscure references from 1840 that I discovered in my searches.

Writing in the Scioto Post, Cameron described, "the activity always picks up and reaches a peak around the Holidays.

There was the time last December when three ornaments flew off the Christmas tree at once, landing halfway across the room. A few nights later, I was in the upstairs hallway when I heard my name being called from downstairs; my dogs heard it too. Knowing no one else was here, the dogs ran downstairs to see who it was. Of course, no one was there.

A couple of years ago, it was my nephew's first Christmas, and there were kids' toys wrapped up under the tree. More than once, the toys started playing music, also singing and moving on their own; it was crazy.

This past Christmas was no different; I went downstairs to find the vacuum cleaner on and running all by itself. Loud screeches and yells echoing throughout the house late at night, these will make your blood run cold. And there's never any explanation.

One night shortly before Christmas, my mom had an experience in her room that really frightened her. She woke up to find the Amazon Alexa device in her bathroom was playing Christmas music. Now, these devices only respond to a person's voice. So, Alexa heard a request to start playing Christmas music, and it did. She got up, turned off the music and after she calmed down a bit, laid back down, and the music started again."

This story is highly unusual, the ancient origins, the tradition of the ghost appearing at Christmas, and then seemingly related to the experiences of Cameron and his family.

Did the ghost of the old Courthouse move home, and what is the link with Christmas? Like all good real ghost stories, this remains a mystery.

The White Lady of Worstead

Can ghosts heal the sick? A little village in Norfolk, England, has a very unusual ghost with seemingly ancient origins. In the Domesday Book, Worstead is called Wrdesteda and Ordested and was in the ownership of nearby St. Benet's Abbey after being given as a gift by King Canute. The Abbots would be known for offering respite and healing to those who needed it, and of course, preaching to the local towns and villages.

Death wandered into Worstead in the 13th Century, and no amount of prayers would stop its progress. Over the next three hundred years, in the guise of the Black Death, families would be decimated both financially and personally, with some even turning to cannibalism to survive.

The first outbreak in Norfolk was in 1349, the year after Worstead's church, St Mary's, was first founded. Over the next year, hundreds of thousands of people died across the county, and Worstead was no different. Two-thirds of the county's clergy and over half the population died.

Out of the devastation of the Black Death, Worstead rose out of the ashes to become a centre of Norfolk's wool and cloth trade.

The building of St Mary's Church continued in the 1350s and was extended over the next hundred years as it became more affluent. For the next five hundred years, the village grew in population with St Mary's as its spiritual and physical centre. Then the industrial revolution curved this growth as social mobility and the 'satanic' weaving mills were able to source cheaper materials.

There is only one ghost that haunts Worstead, and that is enough for this small village.

Depending on who you speak to, they believe she is capable of scaring people to death or kindly spirit who can heal. Visitors to Worstead and St. Mary's at Yuletide may not be aware of this long and varied haunting. The only clue, maybe the pub opposite the church, is now called in tribute to the village's ghost, "The White Lady".

But back in the 1830s, many villagers knew of the story of the White Lady who would appear at Midnight on Christmas Eve at St Mary's Church.

According to one story, at the turn of the 18th century, filled with Christmas cheer (or plenty of booze), a man boasted that he would challenge the White Lady. He said he would climb to the top of the church's belfry and kiss her if she appeared, so off he went. When he failed to reappear, the local townsfolk searched for him. The poor man was found cowering in the belfry, shaking. He told his friends, "I've seen her. I've seen her," and then promptly died.

Over the next hundred years, the legend of the White Lady seemed to drift out of fashion and resigned to the history books but did the White Lady return in 1975?

A young couple called the Berthelots and their son visited Worstead in 1975, and after a visit to St. Mary's church, Mrs Bethelot's life would be changed for the rest of her life.

That day the Berthelots had taken the journey to the village from their home in Essex to gain a little respite. Diane Berthelot has been struggling with ill health, firstly with her gallbladder, and then on that hot summer's day, she was taking antibiotics for an ear infection. She felt overwhelmed by her symptoms; Peter, her husband, took the family for a trip to the idyllic village.

After an hour of walking around the village, Diane, understandably, could not cope with the heat of the summer's day so went inside the church to escape the heat.

At that moment, struggling with her symptoms, Diane said a prayer to help her recovery while her husband and son explored the old church. Unaware that her husband was taking photographs of the church and herself, she began to feel a peace and warmth as if her prayer had been acknowledged.

The Berthelots left Worstead later that day feeling more optimistic, and Diane felt as if she had turned the corner of her illness.

Several months later, the family decided to have a slide show of the holiday photographs taking over the summer. They hadn't seen the photographs since they were taken, and when the slide of Diane appeared, Barbara, a friend, pointed out that someone was sitting behind Diane.

In the photograph (available to view online), Mrs Berthelot sits, head slightly bowed as she rests on the church pew. Behind her is a figure in white, seemingly wearing a shawl and an old-fashioned bonnet. The figure seems to be sitting behind Diane, with her unaware of this figure.

Diane told The Express newspaper, "She said: "When we saw the white figure sitting behind me on the projector screen, we just stood there with our mouths open.

"My feet started to tingle. This sensation eventually engulfed the whole of me. It was a pleasant, comforting feeling." Her husband added: "I had been walking around the church looking at various things. I came back, saw Diane sitting there and took the photo. I couldn't see anyone behind her, but it's so clear on the image. It's incredible."

The next summer, the Berthelots returned to the Worstead church and showed the photograph to Reverend Pettit, the then vicar of the church; he explained the legend of the White Lady and that in more recent times, she wasn't viewed as something to be feared, but a healer of those in sickness.

Interestingly for many years, Mrs Berthelot still experienced the same calming, tingling sensations whenever she looked at the photograph, but that feeling has since subsided.

Max Darbyshire, who lives in Worstead, wrote to one website about the White Lady,

> I used to live in Worstead, an interesting little rural village. The White Lady of Worstead is very popular and has been seen by many people, including the local vicar. I remember as a child that a Fish and Chip van would pull up in the village square by the church on a Friday night, and the man running it would often talk about how he once saw the white lady while he was closing up shop.

> He said she moved between the gravestones and walked through the large doors of the church. He then claimed that a white light seemed to emanate from the windows.

Another time, a friend of mine was drinking with a
couple of friends in the graveyard (don't judge,
rural England can be extremely boring for
teenagers) when he claimed the gravestone he was
seated against seemed to lurch behind him, upon
spinning around there was a woman in a white
dress and bonnet staring down at him with a stern
face. All three of them ran out of the graveyard
and didn't return that night.

Most of us see ghosts and ghost stories as being something to fear.
Whatever you feel about the photograph or the sightings of the White
Lady, Diane's experience touched her, for the positive, for the rest of
her life.

From the Author

I hope you enjoyed my first collection of original ghost experiences and the vast array of phenomena reported by the witnesses. If you would like to submit an experience or was a witness to some of the stories in this book, please email mj@mjwayland.com

For further ghost stories and research as well as my future releases please visit my website - www.mjwayland.com

Thank you

MJ Wayland

My other books include:
50 Real Ghost Stories
50 Real Ghost Stories 2
50 Real American Ghost Stories
The York Ghost Walk
The Derby Ghost Walk

All are available from Amazon and other good bookshops.

About the Artist

I would like to especially thank L.Jeffrey for providing both inspiration to me, and incredible artwork for this book. While a good ghost story can flicker into life in our imagination, I believe the art in this book adds even more, capturing the atmosphere of a ghost experience.

You can discover more of her work at ghestwyck.com and on social media as ghestwyck.

Watch out for our next book together!

The Haunted Caxton Gibbet by L.Jeffrey

Printed in Great Britain
by Amazon